FREEDOM AND AUTHORITY

David Cook

Scripture Union
130 City Road, London EC1V 2NJ

First published 1988

ISBN 0 86201 383 6

British Library Cataloguing in Publication Data

Cook, David
Freedom and authority.
1. Authority – Christian viewpoints
I. Title
261

ISBN 0–86201–383–6

Phototypeset by Input Typesetting Ltd, London
Printed and bound in Great Britain by
Cox and Wyman Ltd, Reading.

Contents

Dedication

To Jimmy and Jenny White
for their love and their daughter.

PART ONE

Looking at freedom and authority

1

The crisis of authority

The church is going through a crisis of authority, as is the whole of our society. The church crisis is only part of a much wider problem and conflict.

At election times we are faced with what politicians call the issues of 'law and order'. Whether we like it or not, we are all faced with laws and orders in society and have to decide what we will do with them. Should they be obeyed? Should they be obeyed without question? Should they be obeyed without question at all times? Behind laws and orders lies authority. The authority of government, of politicians and of the police is embodied and expressed in law.

Our society is witnessing a rejection of traditional authority, and this is happening in the name of freedom. It is important that from the very start we see the interaction and connection between these two ideas. In our society freedom and authority are thought to be in opposition to each other. If I accept authority, then I seem to give up my freedom. If I exercise my freedom, then it looks like a refusal to accept authority. The refusal to accept authority has led to the so-called 'breakdown' of the rule of law and order.

We regularly hear people bemoan the breakdown of law and order, but there are different aspects to this breakdown.

Laws and their officers

First, there is the calling into question of law and the officers of the law. In a democracy we all feel perfectly free to ask if we should have these laws and whether or not a law is good. Well-publicized breaches of trust and abuses by the police have made us all ready to question individual policemen and policewomen, as well as the institution of the police, its organization and behaviour.

Secondly, the rise in crime and violence, the increase in criminal offences and the growing numbers in prison and penal institutions all show that traditional respect for law and the keeping of law is disappearing. This is all the more evident when we think of how people view the police force. The street-wise call the police 'pigs', showing how far our society has moved from its traditional respect for the local 'bobby'. The police seem to be there to be abused, sworn at, pelted with all kinds of missiles and generally insulted and assaulted. Of course, there may be ways in which the behaviour of certain individuals and sections of the police force has not helped this process, but it does not change the fact that the traditional embodiment of law and order – the police – carries little respect and authority within our society.

The family

The breakdown of traditional values in the family context also shows this trend against authority. Children no longer regard their elders as their betters. Children are most definitely not only seen, but also heard. This is not just a question of their dress and behaviour. It is also in the attitude they display towards their parents and those who stand in the place of their parents, like teachers. Parents blame teachers and teachers blame parents for the antagonistic attitudes shown by young people to those responsible for their training, education and upbringing.

The extent of the breakdown of authority in schools has led some teachers to resign, unable to cope with the disorder. The chaos in the classroom is often matched by chaos at home. The failure of discipline in the school setting is equally matched by the failure of discipline in the home. Indeed, the use of corporal punishment by parents against their children is as rare as the use of corporal punishment in schools. This is very far from the old dictum that to spare the rod was to spoil the child. If this dictum is true, then most of us and our children are well and truly spoiled. The truth is that we are no longer sure how to exercise discipline in the home or how to make it effective in the schools.

But it is in the home that the traditional roles of father, mother, grandparents and older relative no longer carry the authority they once did. Age seemed to be respected and to have the right to speak with authority to those who were younger. Now parents, just because they *are* parents, no longer seem entitled to exercise authority over their children. But what does it mean to exercise authority? What is it that authority seeks to do to us, that we are no longer as willing and able to accept?

Education

Authority tells us what to do, and is to be obeyed. But we are no longer ready to obey authority when it tells us what to do; we do not think of obedience as a virtue and we can barely understand people who will obey orders without question at all times. This is because we are *taught* and *encouraged* to question everything.

This process begins in the nursery and kindergarten. The inside of a nursery school often looks chaotic. Children are scattered all round the room doing different things. Some are playing with water, others are in the Wendy House, others are sitting in the book corner, and still others are playing with sand, weights and scales. To us, the onlookers, it looks like bedlam. In fact, it is a carefully thought through philosophy being put into practice. It is called 'child-centred education'; children and young people are encouraged to learn in their own way, at their own pace and according to their own interests.

This carries through into the primary school, where the young person is encouraged to select a topic and discover all that he or she can about it. The children are encouraged to follow their own inclinations and concerns and are not expected to sit in rows or learn by rote. Certainly there is little of the traditional idea of a lesson where the teacher taught the whole class the same thing at the same time.

This process and philosophy culminates in the higher education world of college and university. Parents often complain to me, as a university teacher, that their children have been changed after a term at college or university. They do not see this change as being for the better. The parents tell me that their children used to be such nice young people, always tidy and smartly dressed. They were unfailingly polite and agreed with everything that was said to them. But after a term away, they have become sloppy and untidy. They dress in outrageous ways and disagree with *everything* that other people say. 'If you try to have a conversation with them', the parents complain, 'they end up criticizing everything you stand for and do'.

What have we, the educators, done to them? The answer is very simple. We have educated them! For the aim of education in the West is to make everyone think for herself or himself. The process which achieves this consists of questioning and criticizing everything. Those who do best in Western education are those who are able to question everything they meet and are able to criticize and evaluate the views of others. We teach people how to take things apart without being very good at helping them to put it all back together again.

I once had a Mexican student whose father had left him a theological college. He did not know very much theology, so he decided that it would be a good idea to learn some and so came to Britain. I set him an essay on Christology, 'Who is Jesus?' and gave him one large tome to read. His essay appeared soon afterwards. It was an excellent description of what the writer of that book had said. I complained that this was not good enough. I needed to know whether the writer was right or wrong; I needed to have some critique of the position presented in the book. The student looked at me in astonishment.

'Who am I to criticize the writer of the book?' he asked. A student ought not to criticize such a learned man who knew enough to write books, he thought.

It was difficult, but necessary, to explain to my student that he had to learn to criticize if he wanted to do well in Western education. His views mattered. What *he* had to say – if it was based on good and sound evidence – counted for just as much as anything any learned writer had to say.

We *teach* people to question authority. The best student is the one who is able to question everything. That is the heart of the critical method.

A father once took his daughter to the zoo. They saw the elephants and the little girl asked why they were called elephants. The father said that he did not know. They saw a rhinoceros and the girl again asked why it was called a rhinoceros. The father said that he did not know. They saw the hippopotamus and the girl asked the same question. The father again confessed his ignorance. The girl asked whether he minded her asking all these questions. The father replied that he did not mind at all. After all, this was the only way she would learn!

As far as Western education is concerned, the asking of questions is fundamental to being a well-educated person. The problem is that once you have taught people how to ask questions, they cannot stop. It is a fatal disease. Everything and anything becomes open to question. There is nothing which is beyond question, there are no forbidden areas, nothing is accepted as it stands. Sadly, we fail to see the implicit destructive element in that education process.

Society

We question the institutions and the people in our society which exercise authority over us. The government, the press and the media all have authority in our society, yet who believes what they say? The traditional authority figures – the aristocracy – are given virtually no respect in twentieth-century Britain. The Royal Family still draws a tremendous level of personal support and warmth, but it seems that those members who do not play a significant state or charitable role command less respect. It is not actually clear what difference such respect would make; royalty seems acceptable as a figurehead and focus for patriotism, but it has little or no power to affect how we actually live.

The more localized authority of the policeman or parent seems to be bound up with the general authority of the State. Neither seems to be operating effectively or with any force.

The church

The church is not immune from the trends in wider society. Its ministers and officers have lost the authority they once seemed to have in society and any genuine influence they had over it. Within the church everything is being questioned.

There is a crisis over what we are to believe. Is the faith once delivered to the saints still good for us today?

There is a crisis over what we are to do and the kinds of lives we ought to be living. Are different patterns of human life, sexuality, and society, all to be accepted and pursued?

There is a crisis over what is to be obeyed. The Bible,

tradition, Bishops, Popes and ministers have all been called into question. It is not enough for people to claim, 'The Pope/Bishop/minister has said such and such, so that is the end of the matter'. Authority needs to be defended and approved. It does not seem any longer to be self-authenticating.

The rise of the individual

Despite our rejection of so many forms of authority it is not the case that we operate without any kind of authority. We have filled the vacuum created by the collapse of traditional authority by putting a new authority in its place: the freedom of the individual. It is the freedom of the individual which lies behind the critique of traditional authority in our culture. We have been trained to respond in a positive way even to the word 'freedom', and it is no exaggeration to see twentieth-century life as a quest for freedom. We want to be free from the restrictions that hold us back. We want to be free to do and to be whatever we wish.

In the past we had only four 'freedom' slogans: *freedom from want* meant that we should not live in fear of a lack of food and clothing to survive and flourish. *Freedom from fear* meant that we should not have to live in fear of being imprisoned or harmed without warning and just cause. *Freedom of speech* meant that we should be allowed to express our ideas and outlooks without let or hindrance and without fear of the consequences. *Freedom of religion* was also held to be fundamental for it meant that everyone should be free to pursue his or her own religious and spiritual journey in whatever way was felt appropriate. But these positive freedoms are matched now by our even stronger desire for *freedom from restrictions*. We want to be free from unwanted and disliked pressure, objects and systems. In this sense 'freedom' becomes synonymous with the rejection of authority.

The replacement of authority by freedom has two main roots. The first is an underlying philosophy, or rather set of philosophies, which have affected the ways in which we think and perceive the world. The second is 'history', the experiences of individuals and groups in society which have fundamentally affected our perception of reality and led us to prefer some things to others and to behave in certain ways rather than others. Philosophy and the recent history of the world have radically affected us.

Renaissance, Reformation and Enlightenment

The freedom which rejects authority is the freedom of the individual. This concentration on the individual has its roots far back in Western history and philosophy, but the key periods for our modern understanding are those of the Renaissance (broadly affecting Europe through the fourteenth, fifteenth and sixteenth centuries) and the Reformation (sixteenth century). The old patterns of authority in the church and state began to be broken down and a concentration on the individual arose in their place. The rebirth of learning went hand in hand with the rise and emergence of the critical method of education.

The discovery of ancient texts, especially at the time of the fall of Constantinople, led to an upsurge in the study of Greek and Latin literature. This re-emphasis on going back to the original sources carried over into the study of the Bible in Hebrew, Greek, Aramaic and Latin. But it was found that the ancient texts dated from various periods and were all written in contexts very different from those in which their readers and interpreters now lived. These new readers needed a perspective by which to judge and interpret what was being said in these ancient texts. In this lay one main element of the critical method, that of putting questions to the text and judging what was read by the standards and authority of the reader and questioner. The actual authority used by textual critics was their own wisdom, judgement, beliefs and common sense. Not only was '*man* the measure of all things', but each *individual* had become the standard by which everything else was to be judged. It is no accident that the time of the Renaissance was a time when great artists, writers, scientists and scholars flourished. They were individuals who were encouraged by patrons and by society to do their own thing and the world benefitted greatly.

In religious terms, the Reformation's setting aside of the traditional authority of Pope and priest meant that individuals were thrown back on their own consciences. The spirit of the age is summed up in the words of Martin Luther who is pictured as taking on the might of the Roman Catholic church single-handed: 'Here I stand. I can do no other'. The idealized account we have of what was happening in the Reformation is of the lone individual taking on the rest of the world and winning. We accept this and applaud it for we are convinced that each person has to come to his or her own conclusions and that each of us is responsible for what we do and believe.

Tied into this stress on the individual was the rise of modern science. It is again no accident that the work of individuals like Galileo and Copernicus came into conflict with the authority of the church. These free-thinkers began to question the old and traditional ways of regarding the world. The scientific method of observation, hypothesis, experiment and then the framing of laws, was being formed and refined. While the method was a universal one, it was still for each individual to carry out the experiments for himself and so reaffirm or reject the law suggested. The individual's understanding was the key to knowledge and to certainty. The individual was the standard by which everything was to be judged.

This approach flourished again in the eighteenth century, in the period of history known as the Enlightenment. Great advances were made in science and the arts and there was nothing that could not be investigated or questioned. It was also an age of satire. The writings of Alexander Pope and Voltaire are evidence of the freedom felt to poke fun at everything and anything. Religion, royalty, science and society were all held up to ridicule. No jokes were forbidden, no themes were too delicate or difficult to be handled publicly and openly. No authority was beyond question.

The philosophies of today

Existentialism

The move away from authority and towards the freedom and rights of the individual clearly lies at the root of certain modern philosophies. Existentialism is an approach to life which begins and ends with the individual. It looks at the world around us and suggests that the world is meaningless and pointless. That is, that there is no meaning in anything and no meaning in everything. There is no point to it at all. What then are we to do in such a meaningless world? The solution offered by the existentialist is that we are to create meaning and purpose. Where there is none, we make some. We recognize that this is not ultimate meaning, but it is the best we can do. It is also what it means to be human: to be human is to create meaning in a meaningless world.

This existentialist approach to life goes on to suggest that the crowd is a lie, because it gives a false impression of either conformity or unity. When we are with a crowd of people we do things that we would never do when we are on our own. We say things that we do not mean and we act in ways which are not genuine. When we follow the crowd we live a lie. The only solution is to stand against the crowd and be true to ourselves. We must make reality what we wish it to be rather than simply believe what the crowd says it is.

In the existentialist philosophy of life, the will is the most important feature of human beings. It is the fact that we are able to make decisions that separates us from the rest of reality, whether things or animals. Making decisions, acting in the light of them and taking full responsibility for them is what it means to be an 'authentic' person. While we follow the crowd, or unwillingly submit to an authority other than our own, we are living an 'inauthentic' life. Even to refuse to choose is to make a choice. This sense of the freedom to choose runs very deeply in existentialism.

Whenever I go to London on the train, I assume that no one in the carriage knows anything about me. Quite often someone will ask me what I do for a living. I could say that I am a brain surgeon and am involved in doing brain transplants. It might be fun in the hour's journey to London to try to keep the deception going and to see whether or not the person spots the flaws. In a sense, the existentialist stress on choice suggests that when we meet people, and in the way we live our lives, we are able to choose to be whatever we want to be. We can present ourselves to the rest of the world in any way we wish. Of course, we may not be able to get away with it, but we are still free to choose who we will be and how we will live.

This is also clear in moral issues. The existentialist believes there are no standards of morality which are objective and which we can all see and accept. Morality is, rather, a human creation; we make it and we choose our own morality. We are our own bosses, free to do whatever we wish. Understandably, others may try to restrict us, but that is simply because their choice is to do so.

This is a depressing approach to life. Existentialist writers concentrate on problems which are difficult, almost impossible, to resolve; unlikely and exceptional experiences which a person may have. They then argue from these exceptional settings to how we should live normally. But we cannot and do not live like that. The normal is a world away from the exceptional and we need to learn how to deal with the ordinary and usual before we can have any hope of coping with the exceptional.

In stressing the freedom that each individual has to choose and to be whatever he or she wishes to do and be, the existentialist is uncovering something which lies deep in our consciousness. I remember being at a pool-side in Washington DC and taking to task two young boys for their dangerous and unruly behaviour. The older boy, who was eight, looked me straight in the eyes and said, 'Leave me alone. I am my own boss.' That just about sums up existentialist philosophy. We are responsible to no one else and answerable only to ourselves.

Secular humanism

This is another philosophy which underlies the fabric

of our society. It stresses the secular nature of our world, claiming that we no longer live in a religious society and are in the process of secularization. That process is one in which the beliefs, institutions and practices of a community shift away from presupposing some religious reference, to a society where the beliefs, institutions and practices make no allowance at all for religion or God. So this process carries with it an alternative belief system. God is expelled from our twentieth-century world and humanity is put on his throne instead. God is seen as an old feudal lord in the sky who spoilt things for everyone by refusing to allow us to have a good time. Now that humanity has 'come of age' and we no longer need the support of such superstitions to survive, we are able to take responsibility for ourselves.

At the heart of secular humanism is a belief in human beings and their ability to make it in this world on their own. This belief is also a belief in human reason. While humanity may face many problems and crises, the secular humanist believes that our reason can overcome these issues and find solutions to even the most difficult of problems. Our capacity to think for ourselves will lead to a better life for us all.

This philosophy also believes that our society should be ordered and structured to allow maximum freedom for each individual. As Clifford Longley, the religious correspondent of *The Times* put it:

'. . . the emergence of the concept of the individual is a feature of the irresistible transition to secularism, and to a secular morality based on the idea that the primary moral characteristic of society is the possession by the individual of certain fundamental rights.'

His analysis runs even deeper, however, for he sees that it is not just the issue of rights that matters but also where they come from:

'They are not things granted by any outside agency, or bestowed upon individuals by external authority, but are attached to the status of a single human being as an inherent property of that status.' (2 March 1987)

This stress on individual and personal rights is the very opposite of the traditional medieval way of life. In that setting the lord of the manor had absolute rights over his serfs. The serfs had only duties – absolute duties – to do whatever the lord and master commanded. Our society has moved away from oligarchy, where only a few have rights, to a world where, it is claimed, we all enjoy rights. At the heart of democratic rule is the assumption that everyone's rights are equal.

The individual and the majority

In a democracy, everyone is deemed to be equal, so authority resides in the will of the majority. We agree to do what the majority decides. We do not, however, have referenda on every issue of life because we know society would grind to a halt if we did! The Athenian democracy required *all* free men to vote on *every* matter, and it only survived such constant disruption because women and slaves kept the economy going and ordinary life intact. The free men of Athens were so busy making decisions that there was no time for them to do anything else except relax in the baths and enjoy watching sport. (Athenian democracy extended only as far as free men; it did not include women and slaves.) Our society and our business and commercial worlds would collapse if we all spent our time making decisions about the plans of local and national government.

Yet it must be confessed that the authority of the majority is tainted and by no means to be accepted or followed blindly. So each of us regards our *own* rights and authority as the final arbiter. We feel that, in situations of conflict, the authority and rights of the individual are to be safeguarded at all costs. We like the picture of the little man taking on the faceless bureaucracy, even if that bureaucracy has been set up by the will of the majority. We like it even better when the individual wins and gives the authorities a bloody nose. In the last analysis, it is the authority of the individual which lies at the heart of democracy. We may allow our individual rights to be safeguarded by the will of the majority, but the only pure authority we permit and practise is that of each of us over ourselves. This is the notion of autonomy: the self which makes its own laws.

We have a picture of the ideal human being: it is of a person who formulates and lives by his or her own laws. He or she is responsible for himself or herself and decides how to live and what rules and regulations to follow. He or she is strong-minded, secure, and lives with the consequences of each decision. This requires not only intelligence, but the time and space to allow the process to operate. No one pretends that it is an easy thing to exercise authority over one's own life, but it is regarded as both the most positive decision and the least offensive.

The difficulty for each individual is the sheer load of responsibility. There are lots of different ideas and authorities floating around in every society and our problem is that we have to choose between them. We may not easily be able to sort out the good from the bad. In fact, the ideas which often carry the most weight are not those which are best for us as individuals or as a society, but those which are forcefully presented. So, by maintaining a democracy, we make ourselves vulnerable to ideas and approaches to life which threaten the well-being of that democracy. It is only because the setting is democratic that such ideas can be propounded and discussed.

An example may help to illustrate how vulnerable we become. In a democracy we are to be open to alternative ideas; we are to be tolerant of other people and their approaches to life. That might mean being tolerant of those whose ideas and attitudes are intolerant. You are walking down the main street feeling that you are a tolerant human being. God is in his heaven and all is well with the world. Suddenly, a crazed person grabs you by the lapels, stares in your face, and asks, 'Have you seen any tolerant people today?' You are just about to tell him that this is his lucky day because he had just happened to bump into you – tolerance personified. But you don't get this far because he carries on, saying, 'You see, there is one thing I cannot stand. It is tolerant people. Whenever I meet a tolerant person, I kill him.' At this point, there is a slight hesitation in your mind. Are you willing to admit to the fact of your tolerance and put your life at risk? Does it seem better to keep quiet?

The problem for tolerance is how it copes with intolerance. True tolerance will have to allow intolerance to continue, unabated and unchecked, otherwise the tolerant person himself becomes intolerant of anyone who does not share his ideal of tolerance. So the real crunch comes when the intolerant person is intolerant of tolerance. If the man in our illustration had confessed to being tolerant he would have met his end – which would also have been the end of tolerance. If we are to be truly tolerant, we must say we will tolerate the destruction of that tolerance.

Autonomy and adolescence

There are major problems in a society where each idea

has the same freedom of expression as every other and each of us is expected to take responsibility for ourselves. But we must not exaggerate the difficulties of autonomy. In adolescence we pass through a process which is really a growing into autonomy. We do not arrive in the world as fully responsible, self-determining, law-making and law-abiding individuals. We learn how to become that kind of person. The process of education, as we have already seen, plays a crucial part in that process. But there is also a natural biological and social process which is part of human maturation.

Adolescence is that period of our lives where we grow up and are required by society, as well as desire on our own account, to make decisions for ourselves. Parents and their maturing children are often divided over issues such as when young people should be home in the evenings, where they go, what they wear, who they are with and what they are free to do. Yet there seems to be no substitute for that painful process. The parents have to recognize that their authority cannot continue over a young adult in the way it has done over a child. On one hand the children are increasingly questioning the parents' authority and decisions, and on the other the parents have to begin to let go of the process of decision-making on behalf of another. Parents have to allow their children to grow into full adulthood, part of which is to take responsibility for oneself and to make one's own decisions.

The young person, too, has a crucial part to play in this process. What can a young person reasonably decide for himself or herself, especially if he or she is dependent on parents for housing and finance? We cannot side-step the issue by declaring that eighteen is the legal age for handing over all responsibilities to a young person; being eighteen does not mean that we are infallible and sensible, whereas at seventeen years and three hundred and sixty four days we are still silly and unreliable. Parents and others recognize that there is a stage of physical, emotional and mental maturity which needs to be reached before young people may be free to get on with their own lives. Part of this centres on the capacity to think about the issues, to weigh up the alternatives in any given situation, and to have the ability to think through the principles involved. The other side of the coin is a willingness to accept responsibility. Part of what it means to be adult is to be able to accept blame and live with the results of our actions and choices. Most of us, of course, are very good at trying to escape from the results of what we have done, but adulthood involves accepting that we carry the can for what we do and say, and accepting that no one else ought to do that for us.

The process of adolescence is a painful one, often marked by strong swings of emotion between the extremes of behaving like little children and being terribly mature men and women of the world. Rebellion against authority has a hand in the process, and may be expressed in rebellion against parents, teachers and the powers that be. Often those in their late teens seem to enjoy being contrary and 'bloody-minded'; 'opposition' seems to be their basic principle. It is obviously unhealthy for someone to be always in opposition to everything and everyone, unwilling or unable to take a positive role. But rebellion is used by young people as a crucial way of establishing how far they can go and how far they ought to go. It is only when we know where the limits are and where we currently stand in relation to them that we can then decide where we want to be in future. We all need the firm ground of authority to help us decide this.

Autonomy and authoritarianism

There is, however, another kind of reaction against authority which arises not so much from the growing maturity of the young, but from the abuse of authority on the part of those who exercise it. This is where authority has been replaced by authoritarianism. Bad experiences of authority make us extremely hesitant about accepting any authority other than our own. We know when we have been unjustly treated by authority and where it has taken advantage of its position in order to achieve its own ends. In such cases we have simply been used and abused by a system which was meant to protect and care for us and has done the exact opposite.

Sadly, the bitter experiences of authoritarianism are so deep and overwhelming that they leave indelible scars. Those who have been abused as children know only too well the way in which parents have not given protection but have used their authority for their own selfish emotional, physical and sexual ends. The pattern is all too often repeated in the next generation, raising the suggestion that, if our own experience of authority is a bad one, then we fail to understand the real purpose of authority and do not exercise it ourselves in a responsible way. We all know from our own experience occasions where teachers have used their position as teachers to put someone down, to refuse to answer a proper question, to make a fool of someone or to force a group to do whatever the teacher wants, even if it is unreasonable. What makes it all the harder is that there is usually no means of questioning such authority and no recourse to justice. Such feelings of helplessness at the hands of teachers and others who exercise power over us unjustly, can make us feel extremely negative towards all those in authority. Any exercise of authority which allows no room for question, and is answerable to no one, does harm to those under it and leads to authoritarianism.

Authoritarianism is the exact opposite of democracy. It claims that orders are to be obeyed without question and that those under orders have no rights at all. They are simply to do what they are told. Such abuse of authority is clearly a direct threat to human liberty and freedom, and does not stop with parents and teachers. It is of course typical of many governmental and religious authorities. The story of history is an account of the abuse of authority by governments and churches. With such a bad record, it is no wonder that people are hesitant about investing too much authority in government or religious leaders without making sure they retain some kind of control, restraint or answerability.

Nevertheless, it is not possible for us to do without authority altogether. We still need policemen, governments, Popes, priests, teachers and parents. How then can we understand authority and its proper exercise? How can we understand the true nature of freedom? How can we bring together the language and experience of rights, freedom and authority so that we can live with each other and with all these aspects of our life in their proper places? At the very least, we shall have to explore the nature of freedom and of authority.

2

What is freedom?

We live in the age of the expert. The expert makes the complicated simple. The danger is that instead of supplying a simple solution, the expert may provide a simplistic solution. As the complexity of life grows so we long for simple solutions to difficult and complex questions. The media provide us with instant expertise on the great political, economic, social and moral issues of our day. When the Stock Exchange changed to a computerized system it was called the 'big bang'. On a radio programme one stockbroker explained to the whole British nation in three minutes what had taken the Stock Exchange two years to organize and will take ten years to get right. All of this instant expertise happens in a few brief seconds, so that our attention span is not stretched too far and the adverts are not interrupted.

Experts, like adverts, work on the basis of slogans. What could be simpler than slogans? Pithy catchphrases encapsulate twentieth-century wit and wisdom. When still a schoolboy I used to attend political meetings and the hecklers were better entertainment than the speakers! To be a good heckler is to specialize in the slogan or catchphrase. A prime example was 'What about the old age pensioners?' To this there is no real response other than 'What *about* the old age pensioners?' This kind of heckling material was used as a way of testing the reflexes and responses of the political hack on the platform. Unfortunately, it often seemed that the questions and the slogans were not meant seriously and could conceal a failure or refusal to think through the issues. Slogans and catchphrases may well mislead us.

The slogan of 'freedom' presents just such a danger. Simply saying the word is supposed to guarantee a positive response. The danger is that the slogan obscures thought and prevents important questions being asked. The slogan 'freedom' may therefore conceal some errors of thought and mean radically different things to different people.

Freedom or anarchy?

The word 'freedom' can be used to describe two states. The first is freedom from constraint, coercion and obstacles, a freedom which is the opposite of bondage. The person in bondage is a slave who belongs to someone or something else. The free person belongs to himself or herself and is at his or her own disposal. The list of 'bonds' that people wish to be free from is endless: freedom from fear and want, inhibitions, petty restrictions, tradition, pressure, obligations and from each other – at least in the sense of undue influence and pressure.

'Freedom', secondly, can mean the freedom to say what we like, do what we like and go about as we please, without reference to anyone else. The problem with taking such a definition literally is that we end up with absolute freedom from everything to do absolutely anything. This is in fact anarchy, 'no rule at all'. But is it actually possible to live in such a way, totally free from all limitations and restrictions?

Freedom and 'can'ts'

'Freedom' may mean 'being able to do and say whatever we wish'. But there are limitations and restrictions in some situations which prevent us from doing what we may wish.

The old song goes, 'Soldier, soldier, won't you marry me, with your musket, fife and drum?' After getting all the clothes that he needed from the lady in question, the soldier says that he cannot marry. Why not? It is because he has already a wife and child at home. This is a *legal* can't.

The teacher asks the pupil to draw a round square. The pupil tries and has to admit that he cannot. Why not? It is not possible. This is a *logical* can't.

If we are told to pick up the spider in the bath and throw it outside, we may reply that we are unable to. Why? We cannot bring ourselves to touch spiders. This is a *psychological* can't.

If we come to a deep ravine on a mountain walk, which drops down to a rushing torrent below, our guide may tell us to jump across the ravine. We cannot do that. Why? We cannot jump twenty feet. This is a *physical* can't.

If we are attacked by a couple of muggers in an alleyway and our companion suggests that we make a break for it and run, we might be unable to do so. Why? The mugger has a gun in our back and has told us not to move or we shall be shot. This is a can't of *compulsion*.

We may be set a problem in a science class. It is to design a travel machine to take us back to 55 BC. We cannot do it. We lack the technical ability and know-how. This is a *technical* can't.

The children go to summer camp and are taken swimming in the outdoor pool. They are told to jump in and swim around. They cannot. Why? They cannot swim. This is a can't of *skill*.

A friend is going to Buckingham Palace. He has been invited to a Royal Garden Party. He asks us to go with him. We cannot. Why? We have not been invited. This is a can't of *opportunity*.

Our workmates invite us to go to the football match with them. We cannot. Why? We have no money. This is a can't of *means*.

At a church meeting, there is a general hubbub. Someone asks you to call the meeting to order. You cannot. Why? You are not in the chair. This is a can't of *authority*.

This long list of 'can'ts' reveals that there are all too many situations where we are not free to do whatever we wish. There are legal, logical, psychological, physical, coercive, technical, skilful, opportunity, means and authority limitations which hinder and restrict us. To be honest, though, we are not greatly concerned about having absolute freedom. Rather we want to be free from unnecessary limits and from force. Our choices, and our actions based on those choices, ought to be made without coercion. The main sources of restraint or limit seem to be custom and tradition, pressure from others, pressure from ourselves, and pressure arising from the duties, responsibilities and network of relationships that we have.

The 'can'ts' with which we are actually confronted are not disembodied ideas which somehow manage to restrict us. They find real expression through people pointing out what is usually done and what is acceptable. The limits also present themselves to us in the form of other people. It may be that someone sets us a model to pursue, or it may simply be that we want to be accepted as one of the crowd. The whole area of fashion in clothes is a good example. We are all dedicated followers of fashion to some extent, even if the particular fashion we follow seems long out of date to younger generations. The expectations, hopes, dreams and fears of others make tremendous demands on us and force us to conform to other people's wishes for us rather than our own.

Of course, we may put pressure on ourselves by having our own ideals, hopes and aspirations. Athletes are always keen to improve on their previous performances and are constantly setting themselves new and higher goals in their pursuit of excellence. What is true in sport is true in so many other settings, where the pressure does not come from outside of us but is an inner drive. It can be a healthy thing or lead to too much pressure and consequent collapse.

None of us is an island and because we live in families and communities we find that these networks of relationships create limitations on what we are free to do. Some of these limits we may embrace gladly and willingly. Other limits may be irksome and unpleasant but are seen as a necessary and inevitable part of enjoying the benefits of family and community life. Being related to others means that there are duties and responsibilities which face us all and make us act and refrain from acting in lots of ways which we might not otherwise choose if we had been left to our own devices. Nevertheless we still seek freedom and liberty.

Freedom and tradition

The cry of the elderly and aging is that things are not what they used to be. The response of the young seems to be a heartfelt 'Thank goodness!' There often does seem to be a struggle between the way things were and are and the way we want things to be. The past may be set up as a limit for what we are allowed to do now. Arguments like, 'We never used to do that sort of thing,' or 'In my young days . . . ' or even 'People don't . . . ' can all be reduced to, 'This is not how things have been done so far'. In itself this does not seem to be a very convincing reason for things to remain as they are, and generations of young people have rebelled against the dead hand of the past being used as a block on their desires and experiments.

The young are adept at developing arguments against this kind of position. 'Perhaps,' they suggest, ' the past was not so wonderful after all; most people seem quite happy to enjoy the good things that change has brought. Would we really want to go back to the good old days if we could? Obviously the past was not perfect, but nor, for that matter, is the present.' However, it is not quite as simple as we may think to step outside of our past and tradition. The past makes us part of what we now are. It shapes us in lots of ways without our even being aware of the fact. We are born into a world of values, roles, relationships, languages and ways of behaving which are already set up for us. We have no choice in the matter. Our parents, relatives, teachers and friends all mould and shape us in conformity with the world. We are made to conform, not necessarily by some evil plot to make us like robots and automatons but because we are in no position to choose to do otherwise. Moreover, we are totally dependent on that world for our survival, and if we are to continue to survive in it we must initially accept it and try to understand how it functions. Only then can we even begin to think of changing and adapting it.

Inevitably, there comes a time when we are able to question that world, its values, its standards and its impact upon us. We begin to ask whether we should conform to that world, and why. We search for alternative values. We want to be free from the past. Yet the deep influence which our world has had on us is virtually impossible to eradicate, it has shaped us so much. As a teacher and lecturer I try to encourage my students to be critical in the good old Western tradition. To make them critical, I teach them to ask questions like 'How?' 'Why?' 'On what evidence?' and most of all, 'So what?' The really hard thing is to teach them that to take the lessons to their logical conclusion they must also learn to criticize their own teacher's work and teaching. This sounds a rather noble, selfless act on my part, but it is a bit more complicated than that. In order for them to be critical of my teaching they have to use the very questions and critical tools that I myself taught them. So they are not really totally free in their critique, but are limited by the ways in which they have been taught and the tools they have been given. This is not some dastardly plot on my part to ensure that I remain their teacher and they my students. It is an inevitable fact of the teaching process. Naturally, I would be delighted if they were able to go far beyond what they are taught. There may well come a point where they do produce new critiques and questions for themselves which are truly original, but it is rare and it is almost impossible for us to be set free from the limits of the education we have been given.

In the same way we cannot step outside the world, which has been shaped by the past and tradition. We have no point on which to stand to question that world, its past and its tradition. We *do*, of course, question these things, but the process of questioning and doubting is a much more complex affair than we imagine. Our freedom from the past is much more limited than we think. In this sense, the search for absolute freedom is a lost cause. Freedom is always a freedom within limits. Without such limits it is possible that the notion of freedom would not make very much sense at all. It would certainly not relate in any way to the situations we face and the limited freedom with which we have to learn to work.

Freedom and pressure

We are often pressurized, by our situation or by other people, to do certain things. This impinges on our freedom in a crucial way. If we are forced to do something, not only are we not free, neither are we fully responsible for the action we carried out under duress. The person who shoots someone else and kills them while a knife is being held at his beloved's throat may be guilty of manslaughter, but not of murder. The use of coercion makes a major difference to how we regard a particular action. While the pressure of physical violence is an obvious one, there are many other pressures on us which are much less blatant yet still affect our freedom.

First, there is *pressure to conform*. Parents often find it difficult to understand their children's desire to exchange the slavery of the parent's way of doing things for the slavery of their friends' way of doing things. In the name of freedom we might simply exchange one kind of slavery for another. Our friends, our peer group, our social contacts, our workmates, our church groups, our neighbours and our families all create pressures on us to conform. It is not always easy to sort out what it is that *we* want and what it is that *others* want us to do and be. The pressures can be subtle, hardly recognizable as pressure at all: fashion, advertisements, jokes and manners are all presented as normal, ordinary parts of life. They are portrayed and we are confronted by them. We pick up suitable and unsuitable ways of dressing and behaving without even noticing that we are learning anything different from what we already know and do. Many of these pressures are so much part of our cultural setting, and of our understanding and experience of normality, that we imbibe them as we breathe the air we need. As the old Chinese proverb expresses it, 'If you want to know what water is, do not ask a fish'. To be totally surrounded by the medium in which we all live is to be largely unconscious of its impact upon us.

Secondly, *our responses are not always made freely*. All too often, to say 'No' to one pressure is to appear to be saying 'Yes' to a different one. It may also be that we are actually being pushed in one particular direction by the pressures around us. Again, none of us is free from the pressure of other people. Their personalities, styles, communications and the way in which they relate to us make us respond consciously or unconsciously to the pressures they bring. Any of these responses may be good, constructive and helpful. They can equally be negative, limiting and diminishing. This largely depends on how we perceive the pressures and, indeed, on whether we are aware of them in the first place.

Thirdly, some might argue that we are still free to be ourselves. But we are not simply victims of other people and their pressure on us, we may also be *victims of our own selves*. We may be victims of our backgrounds, inhibitions, personalities, hopes and fears. We may be the way we are because our experiences of life have shaped and moulded us to that particular form. In contrast, the 'free to be ourselves' lobby assumes that we all *understand* and know ourselves and what we want, as well as being *able* to fulfil these wants and desires. It is not quite as simple as that. Who and what we are is never some fixed sum of qualities which is given and unchanging. Our feelings and attitudes vary enormously according to our situation and understanding. They often change with time. We vary in the ways in which we relate to different people, so much so that others may wonder if it is really the same person who is being described by two mutual acquaintances. We are often inconsistent in the way we behave to others; we are not always the warm, loving and accepting people we might long to be. Our moods and reactions vary with the weather, our general state of health, our recent experiences and our current view of ourselves. We are not necessarily totally consistent about our attitudes towards ourselves. At times we may like ourselves and think that there is no one else quite like us, so we act as if we are the most important person in the world. At other times, we truly despise and hate ourselves and are not interested in taking even a minimum of care for ourselves.

Freedom, as we see here, is a slippery concept. The notion of freedom only really seems to make sense when seen against a background of restraints and limits. If we have known no rules, it is very hard to know what freedom from rules means. If we have known nothing but rules, it is equally hard to know what freedom from these rules would mean. In a sense, freedom seems to lie somewhere between the two extremes of no rules and only rules. It is both a freedom from restrictions and a freedom to do, act and speak as we wish. The emphasis is on the individual and his or her wishes, each of us being able to decide for ourselves what it is we do want, as well as being able to meet those needs and wants. This leads us back to the question of what authority we have at all. Before we can answer that, we need to be clear about the nature of authority.

3

Who has authority?

The original notion of authority derived from the role of the author, causer, originator or doer. Authority rests in the one who initiates or begins something. It is as if the originator has the right to some say over what has been originated by him or her. The causer is the one who is responsible for what has been caused. The doer has the power over what has been done. We do not need to explore the notion of authority very deeply before we arrive at this idea of power.

Those who have and exercise power are those in and with authority. Authority is not merely some legally defined power. It is really the power derived from office, character or prestige. If people make claims to have or to be an authority, we would expect them to be able to defend such claims in terms of the office or position they hold, the kind of character they have, or the prestige and standing with which they occupy some role. This prestige usually relates to such things as experience, knowledge, achievements or originality. If people have done something or been somewhere that most of us have not done or been, if they know things or have discovered things that the rest of us do not know, if they have achieved heights of human performance that escape the majority of humanity, or if they come up with some piece of work or thought which is totally unique and original, then they are recognized as authorities.

Exactly the same basis of authority may be present and recognized by others, even where there is no direct *claim* to have or be an authority. Other people may perceive authority and endow individuals or groups with authority, even where there is no desire or attempt to claim authority. The grounds for such an ascription of authority might be exactly the same as the grounds for claimed authority. It is the standing, nature or role of the authority, which is the key.

Authority of office

Leaders, governments, parents, teachers and officers of the law are the kind of people whose authority rests in the offices they hold. Of course, they may also have personal qualities and characteristics which elicit the response of giving authority over and above that which is due them because of their office, but the beginning of authority in these situations lies in the offices held. Authority and power are invested in them because of the role they are expected to play in a particular culture and society. Usually these roles are clearly defined in terms of certain duties and responsibilities. These duties and responsibilities are part and parcel of the job. They go with it and are the basis of the expectations others have of those who fulfil those roles. In other words, it does not matter which particular person happens to occupy a certain role. The expectations and duties are still the same because they are a function of the *role*, not of the individual who happens to be in that role. Authority settings like this work, not because of the person who gives the role but rather, because everyone understands the situation, knows what is to be expected from the one who is in authority, and knows what is expected from those who are under such authority.

In the past, these office holders were there for a whole variety of reasons. The aristocracy, for instance, might *inherit* their roles of authority. Others, such as governments, might have *won* the authority role by success in a power struggle. Others might have shown that they are fit for an office by their *exploits, achievements or training*. Sports commentators, for instance, have often been highly successful in one sport or another. It is interesting that though they usually begin commentating on their own particular sport, where their expertise is obvious, they often progress to commentating on the whole range of sporting activities. Others might have been *selected* by those who have themselves the position, power and authority so to do. General Franco, for example, selected his successor and ensured that he became the king of Spain. Whether a person is elected or selected to office he or she will be answerable because of it to those who have done the electing or selecting. In the same way as the king was responsible to the kingmakers, modern elected officials are responsible to those who have chosen them to fill the office and to fulfil the role that goes with it.

Politicians must put themselves up for re-election and re-selection in a democratic society. If teachers, policemen and policewomen, judges or magistrates do not fulfil their jobs properly, they are replaced. This is what we have all come to expect and accept. Parents, however, seem to fall into quite a different category, for as children we have no choice at all in who our parents should be. Yet while this is literally true, there is a very important sense in which parents are chosen and we can allow or forbid them to play the authority role in our lives. If parents maltreat and abuse their children, then the State steps in and removes the children from their parents. In other words, the State is really saying that these parents are not parents in the ways in which they are behaving and, unless they behave as parents are supposed to behave, society will not permit them to fulfil the role of parents.

It is also the case that, as parents neglect and reject their own children, so parents may also in turn be neglected and rejected by their children. Often those who have been sexually abused as children feel that as adults they can have nothing to do with their abusing parents, for the relationship is too difficult and the memories too painful. Yet rejection of parents may not necessarily be based on any particular fault of theirs. There is nothing sadder than the old widowed mother waiting hopefully but unsuccessfully for a visit from a son or daughter who never calls or writes. We may refuse to allow our parents to have anything to do with us. We may reject not just their interference in our lives, but also their participation. We may say we do not think they deserve to occupy that kind of role for us, or even that we do not wish anyone to play that role in our lives. We might simply want to be left to our own devices to be totally and fully responsible for ourselves. We may refuse to allow parents any rights in our lives and refuse their questions, participation, or interest in us and our doings.

This sort of rejection may rest on the failure of our parents to be the kind of people we want parents to be. Or it may stem from our belief that we have absolute rights as individuals to do whatever we wish without reference to parental authority. We may not feel that we are under any obligation to those who brought us into the world and reared and cared for us until we were able to look after ourselves. In this latter case, it is not the failure to fulfil the role of parent which is the issue; many parents are positive and helpful and yet find that they are rejected through no direct fault of their own. Some children do not seem to recognize that their parents, simply by virtue of being parents, have some rights over them.

The power of the child to reject his or her parent is the same kind of power which individuals in any democratic society exercise over those who have been elected or selected to occupy any office or authority. If those in authority do not fulfil the requirements we expect from them, then the office holder will be replaced. The dynamic remains the same. Authority is seen as a gift which requires fulfilment of certain expectations. Where those expectations are disappointed, a change in authority takes place. Because this way of thinking has become dominant in our society, the authority of the monarchy and of establishments like the House of Lords is something of an anomaly. A King or Queen is not elected or selected. He or she occupies the role by right of birth. Likewise, many of those in the House of Lords are there by birth rather than as a recognition of their achievements. This is essentially contrary to what might be expected in a democracy.

The situation remains simply because of the country's deep affection and respect for royalty and for what it has contributed to Great Britain.

The continued survival of the Royal Family and of the House of Lords may also have something to do with the severe limits to their power and authority. Their roles are largely, though not exclusively, ceremonial; the real power lies in the hands of elected politicians and the political parties. Nevertheless, there is a grey area where the Queen and the Lords can exercise authority. It is interesting to speculate on what might happen if there were to be a constitutional crisis in which the Crown and the Lords sought to function in an authoritative way, challenging the political and parliamentary tradition of the nation. For their move to be successful, and for the country to remain democratic, they would need to be given such overwhelming public support that power and authority was willingly invested in them.

Authority of character

A different, though not totally unrelated basis for power and authority lies in a person's character. People who are given authority, or who exercise it, may have certain personal characteristics or personal experiences which form the ground for the granting or recognition of authority. Their prestige in certain areas is such that they are recognized as authorities in those areas. The world of the media provides the best examples of what we mean. Whenever some new discovery or some new event happens, the media wheel on an expert.

Experts, as we saw earlier, are remarkable people, able to explain to the waiting world in a matter of a few moments matters which are desperately complex.

They offer simple solutions to complicated issues, and we rightly wonder whether the solutions they offer are actually simplistic rather than merely simple. We usually believe what we are told by the experts because they are just that – experts. They have attained a level of knowledge and experience which puts them in the very best position to tell the rest of us what we need to know and need to have explained because we do not really understand. The problem is that in any society, it is not only the expert who is given authority by the media and the rest of society.

If we read popular newspapers and magazines we soon discover what pop stars and sports *personalities* have to say about almost everything under the sun. Their views about all kinds of issues are offered, as if we all ought to take note of them and, like good sheep, follow their lead. Simply because they are pop stars and famous, it seems that they have the right to be taken seriously on every issue. We appear to be extending the authority which they have in one area to things which are quite outside their own field of expertise.

This is a difficult area for us all. We rather like people to give us advice, at least in the situations where we do not know the answers. As a teacher, I know only too well the temptation to answer all the questions which my students ask. Often they would rather have clear-cut answers than try to understand what the questions really are! The sheer complexity of many of the issues that face us today often forces us to depend on experts and encourages our natural reluctance to think things through for ourselves.

People's willingness to substitute what they are told for thinking for themselves panders to some of our worst longings. For perhaps all of us enjoy being listened to and taken seriously. We like to have our opinions appreciated and followed. We all quite like the idea of being a guru. The temptation for the expert is to extend his or her area of claim to be an expert into other areas in which he or she has no greater understanding than anyone else. Once someone is seen in a position of authority it is often difficult to see them in any other light. All that he or she says carries equal weight.

Knowledge and experience give people power and authority over others. We may not all have first-hand knowledge of the attributes of such people, so politicians and stars are packaged in ways which are designed to make the rest of us accept, trust and follow them. The key to the success of this packaging is still, however, the presentation of a certain kind of character, the kind which we recognize as being trustworthy and reliable and so endow with authority over us.

Authority of prestige

As we have seen, this authority of character may lie not so much in the qualities possessed by individuals, as in their achievements and experience. Those who have walked on the moon may not be very trustworthy characters in themselves, but would still enjoy a place of honour and prestige for their achievement. We might still want to hear and meet them, regardless of what kind of people they happen to be. Their past makes them fascinating to us and gives them the authority of a rare experience.

We value those who have outstanding gifts and have used them to achieve unusual things. Novelists, playwrights, actors and actresses, scientists and explorers – they fascinate the rest of us mere mortals. Again problems arise when we expect achievement in one area to lead automatically to expertise in other areas. The Italian elections returned a star from pornographic films to become a member of the Italian parliament. No amount of expertise or achievement in her chosen profession really can ensure that she will be a good or a bad member of parliament. To gain respect and authority in that new setting, she must show success in this new area of life and work. The prestige earned in one area cannot be automatically transferred to another.

These examinations of the nature of freedom and authority have tried to unpack something of how we think about these things in our western democratic society and in the world of the twentieth century. The Christian is not content to leave the analysis there. The question of what the Bible has to say on these themes is crucial to believers. After such an examination, we shall be able to ask whether or not there is a gap between what the Bible says and how we now think and act and what we believe. What we are to do, if such a gap exists, will be an important question we then need to answer.

PART TWO

Looking at the Bible

4

The Bible's teaching on authority

The whole of the Bible's understanding of authority rests on an understanding of God. Who God is and what he does, is at the very heart of the Christian concept of authority. A tour through some of the key moments of God's dealings with humanity will reveal how the biblical writers understood authority and tried to walk in God's ways.

Authority and creation

The authority of the author

As the very word 'authority' contains within it the notion of author and originator, so the beginning of the Bible and its account of God's relationship with the world and humanity rest on God's authorship of all reality. 'In the beginning God . . .' sets the scene that God is before all things, and makes clear the context in which everything else is to be understood. It is in the light of God that we are able to make sense of the world. He is the starting-point and the ultimate reference point.

'In the beginning God created . . .' takes the point further by stressing that God created. The opening chapters of Genesis go on to show that God created the world, all that is within it and, in particular, humanity. He is the author and source of the whole of creation. This implies two things. First, that we cannot understand the world and humanity without some reference to God and, secondly, that God has ultimate authority over what he has created.

The authority of the provider

This authority is expressed in his provision for the created world. God is no clock-maker who sets the machine going and then walks away, leaving it to its own devices. God sustains the world and ensures that it continues to function. He is in control of nature, according to the opening chapters of Genesis, and that authority is shown in the order and regularity of the natural world. The psalmist in particular recognizes that the world only functions because God enables it to do so. Without God, there would be no world. It is part of his provision for us. He is in charge of all that there is and has authority as the provider.

The authority of the model for humanity

This same authority is seen in the creation of humanity. Human beings are what they are because it is God who created them. To understand what it is that has been created, reference must be made to the creator. What is made bears the mark of its maker. So understanding the creator enables us to make better sense of what has been created. This notion of 'bearing the mark of the creator' is expressed biblically in terms of a fundamental pattern in human creation: God made men and women 'in his own image'. He made us like himself. We are bearers of the stamp of God.

A key part of what this means is that we are responsible to God, answerable to him for what we do and how we behave. Genesis pictures the harmonious setting of a garden, and a harmonious relationship between God and humanity. The harmony was there because God spoke to Adam and Eve and they answered him. When humankind disobeyed God's initial command, God called to Adam and questioned him. That picture of humanity standing before God to give answer for what it had done stresses the reality of God's authority over humanity and of humanity's answerability to him.

God is the one who has the right to question us. He has authority over men and women and we are answerable to God for all we do, say and are. This itself implies that there are certain moral standards God expects and, indeed, has built into the nature of humanity. Keeping to these standards is good for people and causes them to flourish. This is the way God intended it to be. Disobedience to these standards is harmful to people and causes distress. This moral authority is expressed in the nature of the world and in human nature by the God who made them both.

The Christian can look to human nature and the natural world for traces of God's moral authority. Others outside the Christian faith can also see that people reap what they sow; some ways of behaving are good for people while others are harmful. It is perfectly possible for any human being who reflects on the way the world is and on what human beings are like to arrive at the view that some things are right and other things are wrong. The rightness or wrongness of these things rests in the way they enable people to flourish, or in the harm they do. If the world and human nature are taken seriously, there is some basis for a moral consensus between Christians and non-Christians.

The moral nature of the world does not necessarily, however, point to the authority of God. The link between the two is not established unless there is a clear recognition of the fact of creation and of the nature of the creator. The evidence alone is ambivalent. So, while we may disagree about the authority which lies behind the moral nature of the created world and of human nature, there need be no disagreement about the reality of authority. Morality, however, has close links with the notion of authority.

The Christian believes that the ultimate basis of moral authority is God. This is seen in the Genesis account where God sets certain standards for human living. In the Garden story, Adam and Eve are forbidden to eat the fruit of the tree of knowledge of good and evil. Law, moral standards and the difference between right and wrong come into the world by the command of God. In the giving of the command no justification is offered or demanded. It seems enough that God himself gave the command. He is God. The sole authority lies not in the command itself, but in the giver and his authority.

The man and woman break the command. They do exactly what they are forbidden to do. They set their own authority over and aginst God's authority. From the very start, even in a perfect garden setting, human beings question and come into conflict with God's authority. They think that their own is better. They act on the basis of their own judgement and authority, rather than being willing to accept God's authority expressed in his command.

The results are drastic. We call this 'the Fall'; human beings, in their relationship with God, with each other and with the world in which they live, are fundamentally affected. When Adam is called to give an account before God of his behaviour, he refuses to accept responsibility for what has happened. This in itself is a mark that what has taken place is an abuse of authority. Authority and responsibility go hand in hand. The failure to accept responsibility reveals the lack of proper authority.

Adam blames Eve and then goes on to blame God himself, 'The woman you put here with me ...' (Genesis 3:12). In his excuses, Adam tries to claim that the authority behind his actions was not his own – it was either Eve's or God's – so the responsibility and blame are not his own either. The story of the Fall illustrates the nature and basis of authority in the world. God is the source of morality and the ultimate moral authority. He sets the moral standards. Humankind is required to acknowledge that authority and to give God his rightful place. Failure to obey God's will is a refusal to recognize God's authority.

This rejection of authority has serious consequences for humanity and the world; the authority inherent in God by virtue of his authorship of the world is not something that affected only the ancient Israelites. Similarly, the answerability of Adam and Eve was not unique to them; the early chapters of Genesis show that the whole of humanity is answerable to God. The world has been made in such a way that to disobey God's authoritative command leads to disaster, disunity and disarray. Authority is good, and the acceptance of God's authority leads to the good of human beings. Rejection of it leads to disaster. The acceptance or rejection of authority is not a 'take it or leave it' matter. It matters vitally to the well-being of all humankind.

Authority and covenant

The history of the people of Israel is marked, from the garden of Eden and the time of the Fall, by covenant. A covenant is a two-sided agreement. Both parties agree to enter into a mutual relationship. Each has a specific role to play and obligations to fulfil. In return for fulfilling those requirements each will receive certain benefits. The mark of the relationship between God and his people is that God takes the initiative in making the covenant; God makes various promises to his people and they agree to live as God intended them to. Both sides agree to keep their side of the bargain.

This way of describing the covenant relationship makes it sound like a business deal but it was intended to be a personal commitment of love. Genesis is full of such covenants of love and grace which God made with humanity. In the covenants God made with Noah and Abraham he set out his authoritative will and plan for the future of humanity and especially for his people Israel.

The story of the flood starts off with a challenge to the authority of God by human wickedness. The flood was the means of restoring his authority among humankind and of expressing his moral nature; God takes sin very seriously and responds to wickedness. But his judgement is righteous and he preserves what is good in his creation. Representatives of humanity and the animal creation are preserved. The slate is wiped clean and humanity is given another opportunity to live as God intended, following God's authority. To express this new opportunity God and Noah enter into a covenant relationship, and a rainbow is given as a sign and reminder of it. On his part, God promises that he will never again destroy the earth by a flood. On man's part, humanity is given the whole of creation for food, but with one key restriction, 'And for your lifeblood I will surely demand an accounting. I will demand an accounting from every animal. And from each man, too, I will demand an accounting for the life of his fellow man' (Genesis 9:5). This restriction is a reminder that men and women are made in the image of God; they are moral beings and are answerable to their creator. God intends them to live in certain ways to fulfil their humanity. God's moral demands on us are going to make a difference to the way we all live together.

Jewish people look to Abraham as the father of their nation. The promised land motif, which runs throughout the Bible, comes from the stories of Abraham and is significant not just for Jews but for us all. In making the covenant with Abraham, God made it quite clear that all nations will be blessed through Abraham. The whole of humanity is affected by God's covenant with Abraham. God's authority, and his willingness to bless, are universal. When Christ came he held open the opportunity for all people to enter into a covenant relationship with him. At the heart of the covenant, too, is the recognition of the authority of God and the willingness to accept that authority. Obedience is the appropriate response to the command of the living God.

Authority and Law

The next most significant moment in God's dealings with his people comes when he gives the Law to Moses on Mount Sinai. This Law is set in the context of covenant. To understand it we need to see it in the light of the Passover and Exodus.

On the night of the first passover God promised the Hebrew people protection from death if they obeyed his instructions – their obedience would demonstrate their faith in his trustworthiness. The Exodus from Egypt was part of God's continuing provision for his people. It also showed that his purposes do indeed come to pass. At the centre of the exodus story there is a conflict between God and Pharaoh. Moses is chosen to be God's representative in that epic struggle. It is a straight conflict between God's will and the will of Pharaoh. God's demand of Pharaoh is to let his people go. Pharaoh refuses and the plagues result. At last, Pharaoh is forced to recognize the power and authority of the living God and allows the children of Israel to escape from their captivity in Egypt into the wilderness.

There is another level of importance which we must not miss in this story. Pharaoh discovered that the authority of the God who delivers his people is not to be questioned, but obeyed. Disobedience of God had serious repercussions for Pharaoh and his armies. But this realization opens up the awful possibility that the very people who are delivered and freed might themselves fail to accept the authority of the God who brought them out of Egypt.

The issue is that of how fallen men and women are to live in a fallen world. In revealing the law at Mount Sinai, God showed human society, in a way it could understand, his standards for human living. The central part of this Law is what we call the ten commandments. These are rules for living in relation to God and in relation to other people.

If we were to examine the legal, religious and moral codes of a whole variety of cultures across the world we would not find endless variety. Rather, we would see that the variety is really a variation on a set of themes. There is a common core of morality which finds expression in the ten commandments. The difference is that the latter is set firmly in the context of a relationship with God. It therefore seems possible to follow or at least be aware of the common core of morality, and know that it is good for people. But the Bible would also suggest that these moral laws are not a haphazard affair or the mere products of chance. Rather they are designed and presented by the living God who is concerned for his creatures and creation.

In this way, the Bible teaches that these laws and commandments can only be fulfilled properly when we are in a relationship with God. That means we need to recognize that God is the ultimate authority and Lawgiver. He expresses his will in the ten commandments and the appropriate response on our part is obedience. If we do obey then good things follow for us and for our society. If we fail to obey, and do our own thing on the basis of our own authority, then society collapses and we all suffer.

It is hard to imagine what kind of society is possible if there is no proper relationship between parents and children, no preservation of human life, no limits to sexual behaviour and expression, no sense of what belongs or does not belong, and no respect for the truth. Without these as basic minimum standards for any society, there would be no such thing as a society. Chaos and anarchy would be the norm.

God's authority finds its expression in a set of moral laws. They are not arbitrary rules and regulations but show, rather, what is necessary if we are to exist and flourish together. It is no accident that these laws are to be found crossing cultural and religious divides. This again points to the universality of morality and the fact that humanity is made in the image of God. The true basis for these standards is not, therefore, the fact that they work – by keeping them we do flourish – but that they express the will and authority of God himself. Of course he wills our human flourishing, but that must not blind us to the actual ground of morality, which is God himself. As human beings we cannot escape from that ultimate authority of God which challenges our freedom and our wills.

Representative authority

For the people of Old Testament Israel, God's authority was expressed in certain key forms. There were prophets and priests and judges and kings. Together, the holders of these offices and roles were to represent God and act on and with his authority. They expressed God's word and will to his people. At various times each acted as a check on the other. This is particularly true of the work of the prophet, who spoke God's word to all the people but often challenged directly the behaviour of kings and priests.

Priestly authority

The priests were the first of these groups to be set apart by God to act as his ministers. The office of priest was ordained by God to organize the worship and sacrifices of the people of Israel. Aaron and his descendants were the first priests and they operated in the tabernacle. The rules of behaviour for the priests were quite stringent, examples may be found in chapters 21–22 of Leviticus. Those who were to be priests were to be members of the tribe of Levi and descendants of Aaron. They were not above God's law but were expected to obey all the rules and expecially those specifically tied to being a priest. Their characters were to match the office they occupied.

By the time that the Israelites were well established in the promised land, the priestly families were responsible for worship. The main centre of worship seems to have been at Shiloh where the Ark of the Covenant was kept. It is obvious from the description of Eli's family in the book of Samuel that priests were not always what they were meant to be. Their role as mediators, providing the people's route to God and being the vehicle for God's will and word to come to humanity, was in danger of breaking down. The character did not match that required and expected of the office holder. God called Samuel into this situation to be a prophet, indicating that the traditional pattern of a family-inherited priesthood was not in itself enough to ensure that God's word came to the people. Though not of the tribe of Levi, Samuel was called to be a faithful priest as well as a judge and to proclaim God's word to his people.

It is not unusual in any society for those who hold priestly office to have a special place in the community; Israel was no exception. God drew near to his people in the worship over which the priest presided. These priests offered the appropriate responses of sacrifice at Shiloh. The high priest entered into the very presence of God on behalf of the people.

The priests were the mediators between God and

humanity and were therefore to have the kind of character and life which was worthy of a priest of God. When they did, the authority of God was recognized and enshrined in that group of men. But when they failed to live as God intended, then God had to take other steps.

The authority of the judges

The work of the priest was paralleled by the work of the judge who dispensed God's justice and applied it to the people. Good was to be rewarded and the righteous vindicated; evil-doing was to be punished. In Exodus we read of Moses himself doing the work of the judge, and of the helpful advice from his father-in-law to create other judges. The judges worked hand in hand with the priests and, when the case was an important one, the priests acted as assessors as the judges tried the case.

After the Israelites had settled in the promised land, there was a period of disorganization. God's authority was restored, in that situation of discord and defeat, by the judges. They were national leaders who were literally called saviours or deliverers. They were not merely dispensers of God's judgement and laws but also leaders in battle. In peace time they ruled with justice. In war they restored order and led God's people to victory.

There continued to be judges in Israel but their importance was surpassed by the coming of the kings. Samuel was a prophet and a judge but his importance lay in his role of establishing kingship in Israel.

Kingly authority

Samuel was the link between the old pattern of God's dealings with his people via the judges and priests and the new pattern which emerged in the kingship of David. Samuel acted as the judge of Israel in the pattern of the judges of that time. That is, he proclaimed the word of God, acted as a circuit judge and interceded on behalf of the people of Israel who seemed to be increasingly drawn into military conflict. Samuel also fulfilled a priestly role, for it is clear that he built an altar to God at Ramah. It is from here that he did his job and his sons were to be his successors. As was so often the case, the family let him down. Like Eli's sons, Samuel's did not follow in their father's footsteps. Their characters rendered them unworthy to occupy the office which represented the authority of God. This failure, combined with a desire on the part of the elders of Israel to be the same as other nations, led to the people's demand for a king. It did not matter to them that their call for a king was quite clearly a rejection of the authority of God over them and would have serious consequences for the nation. They wanted to be like other nations.

God allowed the Israelites to have what they asked for, but his authority was to be maintained even in the new regime of kingship. Not only was Samuel guided to the man of God's choice, Saul, but he also anointed him, thereby establishing a close relationship between the priestly and kingly roles.

However, even from the start it is clear that this dual relationship and dual authority was at risk; relations were often strained between Samuel and Saul. At times Saul seemed to usurp the role of Samuel and at other times Samuel had to rebuke Saul. This came to a head with the disobedience of Saul as recorded in 1 Samuel 15. As Saul had rejected the word of the Lord so now the Lord was rejecting Saul as king. Again it was Samuel who had the key role to play in ensuring continuity between the old order and the new. Samuel was to anoint the new king, David. He was, for the Israelites, the height and flower of kingship ushering in the golden age of Israel. It was a time of success and prosperity and gave birth to the Jewish hope that God would one day reign perfectly over his people.

Tragically, the kingship fared little better than the priesthood had done before it. David's own family was hardly a model of behaviour for the people. David himself was all too human and fell short of the standards God sets for kings and commoners alike. The authority of God was expressed in the victories of the people of Israel over their enemies, but when the people's sin defied God's authority over them Israel suffered defeat. The net result of the kingship was a divided nation and a struggle between God's way and that of the rulers of the day. When the king failed to do God's will and walk in his ways, then God acted to redress the situation. If the character of the king failed to be worthy of the office of kingship and misled the people of God, then God acted. The conflict between King Ahab and the prophets of God, Elijah and Elisha, illustrates God's challenging of bad character and failed kingship. Ahab had married Jezebel and she had encouraged him into worship of Baal and so into forsaking God. Ahab's story shows a petulant, selfish man who used his power as king for his own ends. He destroyed others and abused his kingly office. He was not worthy to be king.

The struggle is seen in the end as a power struggle on Mount Carmel. The prophets of Baal are challenged by the lone prophet of God, Elijah. It is not just a struggle to see whose power is greater. It is also a power struggle for the hearts and lives of the Israelite nation. God acts in a dramatic way with fire and reveals that he is God and that his prophet Elijah has the genuine authority of God.

Sadly, the failure of Ahab to be the kind of king that God willed was by no means unique. By and large the period of the kings was a time of failure as far as following God's way was concerned. It was only the ocassional highlight, like the reign of Josiah, which clearly revealed how a king should lead a nation and broke the authority pattern of the evil kings. It was Josiah who rediscovered the book of the Law and restored the covenant with God. Otherwise the authority of God was to be found not in the actions or leadership of the kings, but in the voice of the prophets.

Prophetic authority

The kingship led to the division of Israel into two kingdoms and the vulnerability of the Israelites to foreign domination. The Jewish nation was conquered and carried off into exile. The traditional carriers of authority were no longer able to function and were no longer looked to as the source for God's authoritative word. During this time it was the prophetic tradition which kept the word of God alive. The authoritative word of the Lord was delivered to the nation by the prophet, but it was often an uncomfortable word and one which the people did not want to hear. The word 'prophet' means not only one who 'foretells', who reveals what is going to happen before it does, but also one who 'tells forth', one who speaks the message he has been given. In this sense the prophet is a carrier of the word of God who supplies the message.

Isaiah 58 is an example of the way in which the word of God came to the people of Israel as a direct challenge to a particular way of life. It was a summons on the part of the prophet to recall the people to be what they were intended to be. The message the prophet brought was seen to be that of God himself, speaking with his authority and summoning his people back to following his will and commands. When God's authority and the people's practical expression of it in daily living was at stake, the prophet summoned the people back to God and his way.

Often, as in the book of Hosea, the word of the Lord came to the people of Israel in their sin as a word of judgement and challenge. But even in sounding such a warning about the natural consequences of following a certain way of life, there was a strong message that the God who cared enough to warn the people was the same God who loved them and would restore them to their former relationship. The message of the prophet was often a message of both judgement and love.

The pattern of authority in the Old Testament began and ended with God and his will. He expressed himself and his way directly, through chosen, covenanted figures and leaders – prophets, priests, judges and kings. None of these had authority in his own right. Their authority was not intrinsic to them; the only authority which they properly had was that which God gave them. They were representatives of God's authority. Whenever they tried to act on the basis of their own authority, the consequences were disastrous. However, this pattern of authority was inadequate to bring people back into a proper and full relationship with God. Other measures were required.

Authority in the New Testament

The New Testament understanding of authority is summed up in the one word *exousia*. It is used to express the authority and power of the Lord Jesus. The

New Testament gives God's full and final revelation of himself in his Son, Jesus Christ. The authority of prophets, priests and kings had not restored the people of Israel to their initial relationship with God, so God chose to reveal himself and his way fully in Jesus.

We may approach the authority of Jesus at two levels. We may offer a theological description of what is bound up in this notion of *exousia* and we may examine the life and ministry of Jesus to see how the New Testament centres its attention on the authority of Jesus.

'Exousia'

Behind *exousia* is the notion that the power and authority present is *given*. It is a bestowed authority and its origin is in God. So Jesus claimed that his authority was not his own but was to be seen as an endowment from God. Similarly, his authority was not merely human or natural but was divine, from God, with all which that implies for the nature and significance of that authority.

Exousia also implies *freedom*. To have *exousia* is to have freedom. Such authority allows or permits. It allowed Jesus to say or do what was genuinely novel and he could not be judged by previous standards of experience because they were inadequate to show what it was he was revealing.

This authority is also expressed in terms of *legality* and *power*. With Christ this meant that he had both the right and the power to do something. There are times when the law expresses its will, but is powerless to act or to ensure that it is put into action. This is not so with Jesus, for his authority is both that of the one who has the right, and also of the one who has the ability and power to put into effect what is willed. There is real and genuine power in the life and ministry of

Jesus for that power lies in Jesus' nature.

Exousia also means something fundamentally *creative*. The word carries the idea of a message or presence which is genuinely new and has in itself the ability to perform and to be. The power of Jesus, as we shall see, was displayed in his words, by his presence and by the impact and effect that these had. He spoke and acted in creative ways revealing the nature of the power and authority which were given to him.

The picture most used by the Gospel writers to present the authority and power of Jesus is that of kingship. Jesus is shown to be the messiah, the king who comes to rule and to usher in a new reign of God. As the king, he has the right to do what he wishes. He has the right to act and to control, he has rights over people within his kingdom. They are the same kinds of right which any government has over its people, a master has over his servants, a parent over his or her children, or an owner over his property. Authority means having the right to act if willed.

Authority and revelation

The authority of Jesus was bound up with the concept of revelation. The coming of Jesus was literally an unveiling or exposure; *he revealed God's nature and will* to humankind in a way which could be seen clearly. Jesus was God's 'visual aid'. The coming of Jesus also revealed the very heart of God and brought humankind into it. Jesus was the human being we were all created to be. *He fulfilled, and thereby revealed, God's perfect pattern for humanity.*

Jesus expressed this authority in his uncanny ability to reveal what most would rather have kept hidden.

Jesus read people as the rest of us read books. He revealed to the woman at the well of Samaria exactly what her lifestyle was. She was so fundamentally affected by this that after meeting Christ she went back to Samaria and invited people to come to meet the man who had told her all she had ever done. The remarkable thing is that people did come to meet such a man! Most of us would be a trifle more hesitant to have our pasts revealed in such a public way. Time and again *Jesus revealed to individuals their need and the reality of their situation.*

Jesus was also the revealer in that he ushered in a new kingdom. As the prophets of old had shown the people of Israel the way God wanted them to live, so *Jesus revealed the pattern of life required from those who seek to be members of God's kingdom.* It is an upside-down set of values which is to be embraced. The first are to be last. The meek will inherit the earth. The way to gain life is to lose it. The path to glory is via humility. The poor are really the rich. The king of glory is a servant and slave. It is little wonder that people found the teaching of Jesus disturbing and unsettling! At times even the disciples did not understand what Jesus was getting at. The effect Jesus had was to bring people to a moment of crisis and decision. It was hard to be neutral about Jesus, people were either for or against him. People decided to follow him, or they plotted to kill him.

Jesus' authority in his ministry

The words of Jesus

We have seen that authority tends to lie either in the office or in the character, but there are many aspects to the authority of Jesus. Those who met him seemed to respond to the authority of his words and work. From the very start of his preaching ministry people recognized that Jesus was something quite different from the usual run of the mill preachers and speakers. This is summed up in the reaction to what we call the Sermon on the Mount:

> 'When Jesus had finished saying these things, the crowds were amazed at his teaching, because he taught as one who had authority, and not as their teachers of the law' (Matt 7:28–29).

There was obviously something unique about the teaching of Jesus; it was quite different from what the Jewish people were used to. The authority of God was at work in it as it had been in and through the prophets. Yet the words of Jesus were even more remarkable: he made astounding claims for himself. The list of the 'I am' sayings must have provoked strong reactions from the hearers. In John 14:6 it is recorded that Jesus said 'I am the way and the truth and the life'. He said this in the context of a discussion about the way to God and to knowing God, claiming implicitly that he was the unique route to God, the source of truth about God and the secret of life in God. This is simply one of a whole series of claims which Jesus made as part of his revelation: of himself as one with God the Father, of himself as the revelation of God, and of himself as the means of salvation.

The claims Jesus made caused strong reactions. In Mark chapter 2 we read of the healing of a man whose friends had lowered him down through the roof of the house where Jesus was, because the crowd was so great that it was the only way for them to reach Jesus with their sick friend. The Gospel writer records, 'When Jesus saw their faith, he said to the paralytic, "Son, your sins are forgiven" ' (Mark 2:5). The teachers of the law took great exception to what was being said. They complained, rightly, that no one could forgive sins except God. Jesus knew perfectly well what he had done, what it meant and what they were thinking. He told them that this was no accident but had been said and done that people might know that the Son of Man had authority on earth to forgive sins (Mark 2:10; Matt 9:6). The impact on the crowds was much more positive. 'When the crowd saw this, they were filled with awe; and they praised God, who had given such authority to men' (Matt 9:8).

The works of Jesus

Jesus had a remarkable impact on people. He met fishermen as they mended their nets, and tax-gatherers as they worked at their desks, and invited them to follow him. There is no record of any discussion of a contract or what wages or conditions of service were involved. The call came and immediately people left their nets or work-places and followed him.

The marvellous nature of the works of Jesus is shown in his miracles. These fall into three broad categories. There are the *miracles over nature*. The stilling of the storm or the feeding of the four and five thousand are examples which show natural laws being broken and Jesus controlling nature in order to reveal something of his special character. When the disciples, who were terrified, realized what Jesus had done in stilling the storm, their comment was to wonder what kind of person Jesus was that even the wind and the waves should obey him. The provision of food for the hungry and of wine at the wedding feast at Cana in Galilee revealed Jesus' concern for those in need and the way in which his lordship was exercised in an authoritative way over the natural order.

Jesus also performed *miracles of healing*, revealing his authority over illness, disease and even death. All kinds of sickness were represented in the people brought to Jesus for healing. It is clear that not every sick person in Palestine was healed. This was because miracles were signs of God's work and activity, pointers to the fact that God was at work in a much more special way. Healing people was not the main purpose of Jesus' ministry, though it was a logical consequence of it and therefore a pointer to his true authority which extended over sickness and disease. The most remarkable of these healings were those which involved the raising of the dead. The son of the widow of Nain, and Jesus' own friend Lazarus, had their lives restored by Jesus; though, as the story of Lazarus shows, even making people well and bringing the dead back to life did not win universal approval. The opponents of Jesus plotted to kill him after the spectacle at Bethany.

A third category of miracle performed by Jesus is that of *exorcism*. Jesus was able to confront evil and to win in the struggle against it. This was a genuine ministry of deliverance to people held in bondage by evil. In the synagogue at Capernaum where Jesus was teaching he was interrupted by a man possessed by an evil spirit. It cried out, 'What do you want with us, Jesus of Nazareth? Have you come to destroy us? I know who you are – the Holy One of God!' (Mark 1:24.) Jesus exorcized the spirit and it left the man. The people were amazed and had one question on their lips, 'What is this? A new teaching – and with authority! He even gives orders to evil spirits and they obey him.' (Mark 1:27.)

The works or miracles of Jesus pointed to the authority of his person and his ministry.

The person of Jesus

We shall completely misunderstand the authority of Jesus if we imagine it is summed up in terms of what he said and did. The Gospel writers simply used these stories to indicate what lay *behind* those things he was teaching and doing; they were indicators of his unique nature. He was the incarnation and embodiment of authority. Again, this was *exousia* authority; not some self-made, self-generated feature of his life, but a gift from God.

People's responses to Jesus show that they realized that, in his presence, they were in the presence of the divine. This brought people to a crisis point in their lives. When Simon Peter had failed the 'walking on water' test, his response to Jesus was to ask him to leave as he felt the full weight of his own sinfulness. The rich young ruler was confronted with a painful choice and decided to reject following Jesus. He recognized Jesus' authority and sought to follow him, but was unwilling to pay the price. The authority of Jesus is never exercised in such a way as to remove freedom from men and women. It is a frightening thought that people are able to reject the living incarnation of God and to walk away from Jesus. People are never coerced into Christianity by the founder of the faith.

The most telling story to focus on the nature of the authority of Jesus is that of the centurion's servant. Jesus was in Capernaum and the centurion came to Jesus. He simply told Jesus about his servant and how ill he was. In Matthew's version the centurion does not even ask Jesus to heal the servant, but Jesus immediately says that he will go and heal the man. The centurion seemed to be taken aback by this suggestion for he is recorded as saying, 'Lord, I do not deserve to have you come under my roof. But just say the word, and my servant will be healed' (Matt 8:8). There then follows a description of the nature of authority. The soldier recognizes that he, as a soldier, is a man under authority who has authority over others. He is able to give commands to others and they do what they are told. The soldier is expressing to Jesus that he has seen in Christ one who is an authority himself under an authority. All that is required is that Jesus in his authority simply says the word and the servant will be healed. Jesus is surprised to find this level of insight especially from someone who is not a Jew, but is delighted to say the word and then the servant is, at that very moment, healed.

The authority of Jesus rests in his nature. It finds expression in what he says and does, but these are merely expressions of the reality of his personal authority.

The death, resurrection and return of Jesus

The death of Jesus is recorded in the New Testament not simply as an historical event but as something which had cosmic implications and consequences. The resurrection of Jesus from the dead signified that God himself was at work in a fundamental way, fulfilling and completing the ministry of Jesus. After he had risen from the dead, Jesus appeared to various groups of disciples and followers on a number of occasions. It is in the last recorded appearance in Matthew's Gospel that Jesus spelt out the implications, for the church and his followers, of the authority that was his: 'All authority in heaven and on earth has been given to me' (Matt 28:18). Jesus clearly saw his authority as a gift from God. It was an authority over life and death and an authority marked with God's approval by the resurrection from the dead. Jesus' great commission to the church is set firmly in the context of every kind of authority, and all authority, having been given to him. It is because all authority rests in Jesus that he is able to command, and we are able to obey, his instruction: 'Therefore go and make disciples of all nations, baptising them in the name of the Father and of the Son and of the Holy Spirit, and teaching them to obey everything I have commanded you' (Matt 28:19–20).

Though the authority of Jesus is clearly spelt out in the great commission, it is obviously not recognized by all thus far. Yet the letter to the Philippians points to a time when everyone will recognize the authority of Jesus. It looks to the time of Christ's return and to the judgement which will be part of that event. The same Jesus who humbled himself and took on the form of a servant will be exalted by God and given his rightful place of authority. In recognition of that fact every knee will bow and every tongue confess that Jesus Christ is Lord. The lordship of Jesus, so clearly expressed in many places in the New Testament, is the basis of the authority of Jesus. It was so then and it continues to be so in the context of the church where Jesus is seen and followed as Lord.

5

The Bible's teaching on freedom

Freedom within limits

As with the notion of authority, it is important that we look at how our understanding of God relates to our ideas of freedom. I have two sons and every now and then on a Saturday I make them a generous offer. I ask them what they would like to do that day. They can go wherever they like and do whatever they want. The usual reaction is silence. After a while they often say, 'Give us a few suggestions or possibilities, Dad'. They find the dizzy experience of total freedom hard to cope with. When everything is open and possible it may be very hard to decide between things.

In reality all things are not open. We cannot go to the moon for our Saturday outing. While I might enjoy eating at Claridge's, it is doubtful that I will really take the boys on that expedition, unless some rich relative leaves me a substantial sum of money and clear instructions that I am to spend it that way! There is freedom for the boys to make their choice, but it is not an absolute freedom. It is freedom within certain limitations and bounds.

In contrast the understanding we have of God is of a God who has total and absolute freedom. One question people commonly ask is why God made the world at all. Theologians have struggled to express the fact that God did not have to create human beings or the world. He was not forced to do it. There was no external pressure. Nor was he so lonely and sad that he had to have company at any cost. What God's sovereignty means is that God is self-sufficient and totally free. In his absolute freedom he is free to create or not to create. This makes us feel uncomfortable, for we might not have existed. It looks as if we only exist because of the whim of the Deity. 'If this is Monday, I think I'll create a world.'

While we cannot have any grasp of the ultimate purpose behind God's creating of the world, it is clearly revealed that he regarded the world as a good thing and that he saw creating as, itself, a good thing. It pleased God to create humanity and, because he is a good God, that act and his purpose was good. God was free to create or not to create. He freely chose to create and to make the world as it is – or rather was – in the perfect Garden of Eden.

It is clear that God chose to create human beings as we are, rather than something different. He made us in his own image. We are given freedom as part of our human nature, mirroring God's nature. This freedom is expressed in our capacity to make choices and to act on our own initiative.

There are two key things about human freedom which we must note. The first is that it is, in a sense, a different freedom from that of God. He is absolutely free, with no restrictions whatsoever. We are limited beings who live in limited settings. This is not some grossly unfair condition which God forces on us. Rather it is simply part of the difference between being the Creator and the created. By definition, what is created is made within certain limits, not least within the limits of the will of the Creator.

The second key point to note is that God has been at pains to ensure that our freedom is a genuine freedom. Sometimes people ask me why God did not make us so that we always and only chose what is good. They argue that this would make the world a much happier place. It might indeed be happier, but it would be a fundamentally different sort of world, for the human beings there would be very different from humanity as we know it. In that world human beings would be unable to do anything other than good. They would not be free. The goodness would not be their goodness, but part of their programmed condition. They would be robots for goodness. There might be some point in such a world, but it would not consist of free human beings who were able to choose to love and serve God as well as being free to reject and ignore him. The freedom which God has given to us is the freedom to say 'No' to God. We are not forced to obey God or to follow his will and way. Love is our free response to God, for genuine love can only be offered and given freely. Sadly, we also have the capacity to hate God and to try to usurp his place. The created may wish to pretend that he or she is really the Creator.

Paradise lost

This idea of 'freedom within limits' is expressed in the story of the Garden of Eden. God created a garden paradise for humanity and gave them a specific role in that paradise. When God created humanity we read that he made his intentions clear:

> 'Let us make man in our own image, in our likeness, and let them rule over the fish of the sea and the birds of the air, over the livestock, over all the earth, and over all the creatures that move along the ground' (Gen 1:26).

This rule of humanity was expressed in the form of a command:

> 'Be fruitful and increase in number; fill the earth and subdue it. Rule over the fish of the sea and the birds of the air and over every living creature that moves on the ground' (Gen 1:28).

This all sounds like hard work with little in return, but that was not so:

> 'I give you every seed-bearing plant on the face of the whole earth and every tree that has fruit with seed in it. They will be yours for food' (Gen 1:29).

Human beings were given a paradise to enjoy and a crucial role in that paradise. Their life had point and purpose and there was good provision for all their need. They were free in that garden, but had one restriction placed upon them:

> 'You are free to eat from any tree in the garden, but you must not eat from the tree of the knowledge of good and evil, for when you eat of it you will surely

die' (Gen 2:16–17).

The freedom enjoyed by humanity was a restricted freedom. They were free within certain limits. Human freedom is never absolute. The issue at stake was how humanity would use its freedom.

The account of the Fall reveals how we are tempted to use our freedom for ourselves rather than in proper relationship to God. The serpent is pictured as tempting the woman in the garden by sowing seeds of doubt in her mind:

> 'For God knows that when you eat of it your eyes will be opened, and you will be like God, knowing good and evil' (Gen 3:5).

It is the desire to be like God which is the motivating force in the Fall. We seek to replace God's will with our own and our desire is to be free to do our own thing whatever that happens to be.

The result of this freedom was disaster. The close and intimate fellowship which Adam and Eve had enjoyed with God was broken. Instead of meeting God face to face with no embarrassment, their natural reaction was to hide from God and to cover their nakedness, of which they had not ever been aware before. Human freedom, when it involved rejecting God's clearly expressed will, resulted in distancing humanity from God. Adam and Eve also found that there was conflict and disagreement between them. They no longer lived in unity, but found that enmity had crept into their relationship; and the struggle for power, which so often marks human relationships, became clearly evident.

As with God and each other, so their relationship with nature was also affected by the choices they had made. The world was no longer a paradise. That was lost and in its place the world became a hostile setting in which human beings were forced to eke out a minimal existence. They had to struggle to survive.

The first recorded exercise of human freedom was a catastrophe for humanity. It is clear that there is a fearful price to be paid for freedom and the consequences of the abuse and wrong use of freedom are extremely serious. But it seems that some lessons are never learned and that the human lust to be free from all God's restrictions, free to do whatever we want, is so strong that it continues unabated. This was certainly the case with the history of the children of Israel.

Freedom and the exodus

The story of Joseph gives the account of how the children of Israel came to be in Egypt. It was to escape from a terrible famine and initially they flourished and were safe and happy. However, the good times came to an end:

> 'Then a new king, who did not know about Joseph, came to power in Egypt. "Look," he said to his people, "the Israelites have become much too numerous for us. Come, we must deal shrewdly with them or they will become even more numerous and, if war breaks out, will join our enemies, fight against us and leave the country."
>
> 'So they put slave masters over them to oppress them with forced labour . . . But the more they were oppressed, the more they multiplied and spread; so the Egyptians came to dread the Israelites and worked them ruthlessly. They made their lives bitter with hard labour in brick and mortar and with all kinds

of work in the fields; in all their hard labour the Egyptians used them ruthlessly.' (Exod 1: 8–14)

So the free people of Israel became slaves of the Egyptians. Their lives were filled with oppression and injustice. The innocent and indeed necessary choice of going to Egypt in order to survive ultimately led to a situation of bondage and the removal of freedom.

The Jewish people look back to the exodus as one of the key moments in their whole history. It is the moment when God freed his people from slavery and began to lead them to the promised land. It is seen as an expression of God's concern and love for his people. The story has an unlikely hero in Moses. His escape from death as a child, discovery by Pharaoh's daughter and elevation to the status of a prince in the land of Egypt is well known. But he could not escape from his origins and when he discovered how his people were being mistreated he acted. Like most murders, Moses' killing of the Egyptian was a heated response to a situation of violence.

The transition from the role of Egyptian prince to that of Midianite shepherd did not seem any more likely to produce a saviour for the enslaved Jewish people. Nevertheless, Moses was called by God to be part of the struggle against Pharaoh and to ensure that God's people were set free. The clear message of the exodus story is that God's will for his people is that they are not to be slaves. They are to be free men and women. God therefore acted in ways which ensured that his people were freed, and the land he led them to was to be a land of freedom. The amazing thing was that as the children of Israel travelled through the wilderness, facing the hardships there, they were still tempted to exchange their freedom and the promise of a land of their own for a return to slavery in Egypt. Bondage can seem like a pleasant solution to the hardship and difficulties which arise from being free.

When they reached the borders of the promised land the Israelites were faced with a choice and made another foolish mistake. Like all good armies they sent out spies to see what they were up against in the land of Canaan. The children's chorus expresses the point well: 'Twelve men went to spy in Canaan. Ten were bad; two were good.' Of the twelve spies, ten reported that the task of taking the land was far too difficult. While the fruitfulness and prosperity of Canaan were never in doubt, the degree of fortification, the size of the people and the sheer strength of their numbers led the ten to the conclusion that there was no hope. Their recommendation seemed to be to go back to Egypt. Caleb and Joshua presented a minority report. They believed that it was possible to take the land with God's help. Thus the people of Israel were faced with a fundamental choice. God had promised them this land and had brought them there. Would they now take possession of what had been promised or would they go back to Egypt? The Israelites chose to disregard God's promise and, as a result, they wandered in exile in the wilderness for forty more years. They were told that none of the adults except Caleb and Joshua would survive those forty years. Only the children and the two faithful spies were to enter the promised land.

God is a God who keeps his promises, but he also allows men and women the freedom to go their own way and do their own thing. The big mistake we tend to make is to imagine that such free choices are not very significant or important. They are, and they affect what happens to us *and to our families and relationships* in a crucial way. The children of Israel in their journey from slavery to death came to realise that freedom is a genuine feature of what it is to be human, but it is also one which carries tremendous responsibility and has enormous consequences.

Living in the promised land

When the forty years were over, Joshua was the one to lead the Israelites in the conquest of the promised land. By the end of his life the land had been conquered and divided up between the various tribes of Israel. Joshua summoned all the tribes to Shechem and rehearsed to them all that God had done in leading them to this point. It was time now to establish a new, settled life in this land and the people were again faced with a choice. Joshua gave them his advice:

> 'Now fear the Lord and serve him with all faithfulness. Throw away the gods your forefathers worshipped beyond the River and in Egypt, and serve the Lord. But if serving the Lord seems undesirable to you, then choose for yourselves this day whom you will serve, whether the gods your forefathers served beyond the River, or the gods of the Amorites, in whose land you are living. But as for me and my household, we will serve the Lord.' (Josh 24:14–15.)

The people of Israel were quite clear about what they wanted to do. Faced with a straight choice between the various options, they chose to serve and obey God.

It was easier said than done. From the very start the Israelites were easily led astray and they soon began to worship the Canaanite gods and to practise the Canaanite religion. Their freedom soon took the form of licence. They pleased themselves and did their own thing or, more usually, the thing of those around them. All too easily they allowed the world to squeeze them into its mould. The book of Judges sums up the problem:

> 'After that whole generation had been gathered to their fathers, another generation grew up, who knew neither the Lord nor what he had done for Israel. Then the Israelites did evil in the eyes of the Lord and served the Baals. They forsook the Lord, the God of their fathers, who had brought them out of Egypt. They followed and worshipped various gods of the peoples around them.' (Judg 2:10–12.)

God punished this breach in the covenant by sending raiders against the Israelites. Then in his mercy he raised up judges to save the people from the raiders, but this did not change the people's fundamental attitude:

> 'Yet they would not listen to their judges but prostituted themselves to other gods and worshipped them. Unlike their fathers, they quickly turned from the way in which their fathers had walked, the way of obedience to the Lord's commands . . . But when the judge died, the people returned to ways even more corrupt than those of their fathers, following other gods and serving and worshipping them. They refused to give up their evil practices and stubborn ways.' (Judg 2:16–19.)

The situation continued in the same way until the end of the period of the judges. The seriousness of the situation is described at the end of the book: 'In those days Israel had no king, everyone did as he saw fit' (Judg 21:25). Each person did whatever seemed right to himself or herself; they pleased themselves.

This was the net result of their freedom and the extent

to which they broke the covenant with God. But as we have seen already, each decision and exercise of freedom has its consequences and this brought judgement upon the Israelites.

In chapter four we saw that the Israelites were unhappy because they were not like other nations. They thought the cure for all their ills was to choose a king. With a king to lead them into battle, they believed that all their problems would be solved. God allowed the Israelites their freedom to reject his way and his rule. He allowed them to exercise their freedom in having a king, but it was soon clear that they were no better off than before. The problem was not just with the kings, but with the people themselves.

The books of Kings and Chronicles tell of the downward spiral of a nation. The people of God failed time and again to live up to their name. They broke their covenant with God, choosing to please themselves and follow other gods. They were punished and prophets tried to proclaim to them what was happening and why. They tried to show the people how to interpret the bad things which were happening. At times the people seemed to listen and mend their ways, but these were merely temporary aberrations in the general trend. Soon they were back to pleasing themselves and using their freedom as an excuse for licence. Despite all the warnings, the Israelites seemed to believe that they could go on in the same way for ever. It was not to be.

The Chronicler tells, in stark prose, what happened:

> 'The Lord, the God of their Fathers, sent word to them through his messengers again and again, because he had pity on his people and on his dwelling-place. But they mocked God's messengers, depised

> his words and scoffed at his prophets until the wrath of the Lord was aroused against his people and there was no remedy. He brought up against them the king of the Babylonians, who killed their young men with the sword in the sanctuary, and spared neither young man nor young woman, old man or aged. God handed all of them over to Nebuchadnezzar. He carried to Babylon all the articles from the temple of God, both large and small, and the treasures of the Lord's temple and the treasures of the king and his officials. They set fire to God's temple and broke down the wall of Jerusalem; they burned all the palaces and destroyed everything of value there.
>
> 'He carried into exile to Babylon the remnant who escaped from the sword, and they became servants to him and to his sons until the kingdom of Persia came to power.' (2 Chron 36:15–20.)

Pleasing themselves and exercising their freedom against God's declared will led the Israelites into exactly the same situation from which they had been delivered. They had gone full circle from slavery in Egypt to slavery in Babylon. Exile was the consequence of freedom which was used for the people's own sake and not for God's sake.

The Old Testament shows how human freedom derives from the freedom which is part of God himself and is his gift to human beings. Sadly the pattern of humanity's misuse and abuse of freedom has disastrous consequences for all concerned. However, the situation is not without hope, for the loving mercy of God always seeks to restore things to what was intended and to help people flourish as they were created to do. Individuals and nations have genuine freedom, but that freedom is costly: its exercise has serious consequences.

Since the abuse of freedom in the Garden, there seemed to be no escape from the rejection of God and the negative consequences. The Old Testament is unable to offer a release from this slavery to the sinful use of freedom, but looks forward to a saviour who will transform every situation. Jesus means freedom.

Freedom in the New Testament

Freedom in the New Testament is not so much a concept, as it was in the Old Testament, as an experience. In the Old Testament freedom was a matter of making choices and then having to live with their consequences. The New Testament was written in a world where there were already many philosophies of freedom and its writers made much fuller use of the notion. The New Testament often expresses it by the idea of liberty or of liberation as the writers perceived that the human situation is that of slavery. Men and women are slaves to their own sinful natures and thus to sin. They are slaves to all the faults and weaknesses of human nature. They are slaves to sickness and to death. They are slaves to the power of evil, depicted as Satan. Even those who try to escape from these forms of bondage end up as slaves to the means of their escape. Many Jews were slaves to the Law and to the letter of the Law. Christians, too, fell into that trap so the battle for freedom was a complex and difficult one.

Jesus the Liberator

The theme of liberation, freedom and release was at the

centre of Jesus' public ministry from its start. In his first recorded sermon in the synagogue at Nazareth, Jesus echoed the words of the prophet Isaiah:

> 'The spirit of the Lord is on me,
>   because he has anointed me
>   to preach good news to the poor.
> He has sent me to proclaim freedom for the prisoners
>   and recovery of sight for the blind,
> to release the oppressed,
>   to proclaim the year of the Lord's favour.'
>
> (Luke 4: 18–19.)

The ministry of Jesus was that of bringing release to those in captivity. Jesus brought freedom. The healing miracles point to the way in which Jesus set people free from their captivity to illness and disease. In John chapter 5 there is a fascinating account of the man at the pool of Bethesda who had been an invalid for thirty-eight years. He was a prisoner to his illness and to the fact that there was no one to help him into the water to effect a miracle cure. Jesus knew only too well how easily we settle for what we know and become institutionalized. So he asked the man, 'Do you want to get well?' (John 5:6.) The man did not answer the question directly but launched into a series of complaints. Jesus seemed to treat him in rather an abrupt fashion, simply telling him to get up, to pick up his bed and walk. The man did so and was healed. He was released from the slavery to disease which had taken total control of his life.

The ministry of exorcism was equally a ministry of liberation. Some today call this the ministry of 'deliverance' for it is seen as bringing freedom to men and women from the power and reality of evil. The New Testament writers are absolutely certain that we are in a struggle between good and evil. God and Satan are ranged against each other. But Jesus brought victory over evil and release from its power. The New Testament's record of power struggles between Jesus and evil spirits points to the way in which Jesus is able to deliver men and women from the power of Satan and to give them freedom.

The ministries of healing and of exorcism were two aspects of Jesus' fuller ministry of bringing salvation to the world. In a discussion with the Jews who believed in him, Jesus said, 'If you hold to my teaching, you are really my disciples. Then you will know the truth, and the truth will set you free.' (John 8:31–32.) They were puzzled at this and needed further explanation. Jesus continued by saying, 'Everyone who sins is a slave to sin. Now a slave has no permanent place in the family, but a son belongs to it for ever. So if the Son sets you free, you will be free indeed.' (John 8:34–36.)

Jesus saw his ministry as that of bringing freedom from the controlling power of sin in the lives of those who sought to follow him. It is in the cross that he brought about this defeat of evil and its power, paid the penalty for sin, and released men and women from sin's hold over them.

Before we examine how the rest of the New Testament seeks to apply this insight to the Christian life and community, it is important to notice that in bringing release and freedom Jesus never forced that freedom on people. The rich young ruler remained a captive to his wealth, for he refused to be released from it even at the invitation of Jesus. People are never compelled to enter the kingdom of God. They are free to reject Jesus, able to refuse freedom from sin and its captivity. God respects our human freedom and is never in the business of compulsion. If there is no freedom to reject then acceptance is never a truly free act either and it would be robbed of its significance and worth.

The need for freedom

Paul's letter to the Romans contains one of the clearest accounts of the nature of sin. It is evident that all have sinned and fallen short of the standards God sets for humanity. This is a kind of captivity against which we rebel; we find ourselves engaged in a terrible struggle. The good things which we know are good, right and ought to be done are those which we find impossible to do. The evil things which we know to be wrong we still find ourselves doing and failing to avoid. We are prisoners to our sinful nature and, as with the whole of creation, we are in bondage to decay, waiting and hoping for freedom from that slavery and its results.

James Packer sums up the necessity for freedom by describing the extent and nature of slavery. He writes,

> 'Paul makes much of the thought that Christ liberates believers, here and now, from destructive influences to which they were previously in bondage: from sin, the tyrannical overlord whose wages for services rendered is death (Rom 6:18–23); from the Law as a system of salvation, which stirred sin up and gave it its strength (Gal 4:21 ff; Rom 6:14; 7:5–13; 8:2; 1 Cor 15:56); from the demonic power of darkness (Col 1:13); from polytheistic superstition (1 Cor 10:29; Gal 4:8); and from the burden of Jewish ceremonialism (Gal 2:4). To all this, Paul affirms freedom from the remaining partial bondages to indwelling sin (Rom 7:14,23), and from physical corruption and death, will in due course be added.' (Rom 8:18–21.)
>
> (Illustrated Bible Dictionary, IVP)

Freedom from sin

Part of the nature of freedom is that it is a freedom from things which keep us in bondage. Jesus' ministry, in his life and death, was a ministry of bringing freedom from sin. The New Testament sees that human beings are in bondage to a sinful way of life, a way of life which leads inevitably to death. It is the apostle Paul who is able to explain the dynamics at work here. He describes the situation of people before they become Christians:

> 'For when we were controlled by the sinful nature, the sinful passions aroused by the law were at work in our bodies, so that we bore fruit for death.' (Romans 7:5.)

It looks from that as if the law encourages sin, but Paul is careful to explain that we would not have known what sin was except through the law. By setting standards we became aware of what it is to fall short of them. I used to play a lot of squash and racquet ball and thought I was quite a reasonable player until I saw some televised matches. Once I had seen a proper standard I realized how far short of good play I actually fell!

Paul also seems to be suggesting that one effect of the law can be to awaken this sinful nature. He was quite clear that all men and women are by nature sinful, and he expresses this very forcefully:

> 'As it is, it is no longer I myself who do it, but it is sin living in me. I know that nothing good lives in me, that is, in my sinful nature. For I have the desire to do what is good, but I cannot carry it out. For what I do is not the good I want to do; no, the evil I do not want to do – this I keep on doing. Now if

I do what I do not want to do, it is no longer I who do it, but it is sin living in me that does it.' (Rom 7: 17–20.)

Just a few chapters before, Paul argues that the difference Jesus makes is to set us free from sin and slavery to sin. He pictures the Christian as undergoing a process of dying, burial and then resurrection. The old self was crucified so that the body controlled by sin might be made powerless and sin's bondage thus be defeated. But the death and resurrection of Jesus does not just result in freedom from sin. Death, too, is defeated by Christ, and those who follow him experience freedom from death and receive the gift of eternal life.

Freedom from sin and death are the result of God's free grace. The heart of the gospel is that men and women can freely receive eternal life and freedom by receiving Christ. They are not forced to do so or required to achieve some particular standard of goodness by their own efforts. Salvation from sin and death is God's free gift to humanity. All that is required is the acceptance of the gift and the experience of the transformation which goes with it. Paul's advice is clear:

> 'Count yourselves dead to sin but alive to God in Christ Jesus. Therefore do not let sin reign in your mortal body so that you obey its evil desires. Do not offer the parts of your body to sin, as instruments of wickedness, but rather offer yourselves to God, as those who have been brought from death to life; and offer the parts of your body to him as instruments of righteousness. For sin shall not be your master, because you are not under law, but under grace.' (Rom 6:11–14.)

The Galatians and freedom

It was, however, hard for many with a Jewish background to understand the significance of the gospel. New converts were being taught by those whose experience and tradition was entirely Jewish. There was also considerable debate about what aspects of the Jewish tradition should be maintained by new Gentile believers and this often became a bitter struggle to determine the essence of the Christian faith.

In his letter to the Galatians Paul attacks those whom he calls the Judaizers who have been teaching new Christians in Galatia. The heart of the Judaizers' message was that Christians must be circumcised or else they are not fully Christian. Circumcision was the mark of belonging to the Jewish faith and Jewish Christians wished to retain that custom. Paul had some particularly cutting things to say about those who wished to engage in the cutting of the flesh as part of Christian faith. He argued that if circumcision is necessary for Christianity then the law is also necessary. Thus we are back where we started in a religion based on law with all the problems of bondage to sin and death which result. More subtly, we are also back into a religion of merit: people attempt to earn their own salvation or freedom by keeping the law. This is in fundamental opposition to the gospel which declares that being right with God is a free gift of grace and *cannot* be earned by our own efforts. Faith in Christ is the key to being freed from sin and death. The law proved unable to do this for humankind.

Paul's concern was that the Galatians were being persuaded to exchange one form of slavery for another:

> 'Formerly, when you did not know God, you were slaves to those who by nature are not gods. But now

that you know God – or rather are known by God – how is it that you are turning back to those weak and miserable principles? Do you wish to be enslaved by them all over again?' (Gal 4: 8–9.)

For Paul this is no light matter. The gospel itself, as well as the well-being of the church at Galatia, is at stake. He firmly believes that Jesus has brought *freedom* for humanity. 'It is for freedom that Christ has set us free. Stand firm, then, and do not let yourselves be burdened again by a yoke of slavery.' (Gal 5:1.)

In his enthusiasm to defend the gospel from the legalism of the Judaizers Paul does not allow himself to be deceived about the other danger facing Christians. Once free from sin, the battle is not over. It is all too easy to slip back into old patterns and ways of life. The freedom won for humanity in Christ could become an excuse for any and every kind of freedom. If we are free then some might argue that we are free to do whatever we wish. Paul's response is to point out that this is another misuse of freedom. 'Do not use your freedom to indulge the sinful nature; rather, serve one another in love . . . So I say, live by the Spirit, and you will not gratify the desires of the sinful nature.' (Gal 5:13, 16.)

Paul's final word to the Galatians is that those who belong to Jesus Christ have crucified their sinful nature with all its passions and desires. They now live by the power of the Spirit in freedom, and their job is to keep in step with the Spirit.

The Colossians and freedom

The Church at Colossae faced a similar threat to the freedom which had been won for them by Christ.

Colossae was a centre for mystical religions and a whole variety of human philosophies. There were those in the church who wanted to bring these ideas into the heart of the Christian faith; they taught that there was a secret and better way to God than simply through Christ. It was important to Paul that the Colossians should have a proper view of Jesus and of what he had done for them and all humankind. He points out that Jesus' rightful place is as the Lord of creation and the Lord of the church. That means that the Colossians are to be on their guard against any who would teach otherwise.

> 'See to it that no-one takes you captive through hollow and deceptive philosophy, which depends on human tradition and the basic principles of this world rather than on Christ.' (Col 2:8.)

It was quite clear to Paul that Jesus had helped the Colossians to get rid of their sinful nature and had broken their captivity to it. God, through Jesus, had made them alive even when they were technically dead in their sins and trapped in their sinful natures. They were now free but they were beginning to behave as if they were not free. The attack on their freedom suggested that the only way to please God and to know him properly was to observe religious festivals and to follow dietary rules and regulations. Paul wanted to put a stop to this once and for all:

> 'Therefore, do not let anyone judge you by what you eat and drink, or with regard to a religious festival, a New Moon celebration or a Sabbath day . . . Since you died with Christ to the basic principles of this world, why, as though you still belonged to it, do you submit to its rules: "Do not handle! Do not taste! Do not touch!"?' (Col 2:16, 20–21.)

The Colossians had to remember the good news that they were no longer slaves to rules and regulations. There was no longer any need to worship the elemental spirits or to seek astrological direction. They were no longer at the mercy of the few who claimed that knowledge of God was a secret open only to the initiated and was not for all. In Christ they were set free from all that and, as long as they maintained a right view of Jesus and who he was, and sought to live in the Spirit, all would be well. Their freedom, bought with the blood of Christ, was meant to be enjoyed, not exchanged for another form of slavery.

The summons to freedom

Those who believe in Christ and enter into the kingdom of God are called to live a life of freedom. They are no longer to live as slaves of sin and they are no longer to live as slaves of the law. The freedom which they enjoy in Christ is meant to be lived and expressed. Paul and Peter are in agreement about what this means. Peter writes, 'Live as free men, but do not use your freedom as a cover-up for evil; live as servants of God' (1 Pet 2:16). Paul expresses a similar point of view, 'You have been set free from sin and have become slaves to righteousness' (Rom 6:18).

The only safeguard against a return to the life of slavery to sin is to live voluntarily as slaves to God, fully embracing his way. It is as *free* men and women that Christians are called to live lives which are pleasing to God. His law is given in order that we might conform to his perfect pattern of humanity revealed in Jesus. The problem is that we may hear the word of God and do precisely nothing about it:

'Anyone who listens to the word but does not do

> what it says is like a man who looks at his face in a mirror and, after looking at himself, goes away and immediately forgets what he looks like. But the man who looks intently into the perfect law that gives freedom, and continues to do this, not forgetting what he has heard, but doing it – he will be blessed in what he does.' (James 1:23–25.)

Christians are called to live in freedom. True liberty is found in willing conformity to God's wishes for humanity. In Jesus we see what such a life entails and we are meant to follow his example and so become like him.

The danger of freedom

We have already seen that one set of dangers in being set free from sin is to fall back into a slavery to the law, which can only bring despair and death. The Colossian Christians fell into another form of slavery, slavery to the elemental spirits, dietary laws and regulations, and festival observances. As human beings we seem to prefer being told what to do rather than working out for ourselves what we actually want and then trying to achieve it. But there was another danger which dogged the early Christians as they willingly and gladly embraced the freedom to be found in Christ. This was the danger of licence.

Many Christians in Corinth were using their freedom as an excuse for doing whatever they wished. It was an excuse for unloving licence. Some bright sparks justified themselves by arguing that if more sin was present in their lives more of God's grace could be seen to be at work too! This could only reflect well on God; in fact, it looked as though they had a responsibility to sin more in order to produce more grace! Paul quickly bashed that on the head. If we are dead to sin then we cannot carry on living a sinful life. It would be unnatural to the Christian; a mark that he or she was not really a Christian at all.

But there is a real tension here in the Christian life. Through the centuries it has led to antinomianism. This is the belief that there are no laws for the Christian; everything is permitted and allowed. Paul himself picks up the phrase: ' "Everything is permissible for me" – but not everything is beneficial. "Everything is permissible for me" – but I will not be mastered by anything.' (1 Cor 6:12.)

It is evident that our freedom in Christ is never to be abused and that freely accepted limits to freedom ensure that we are genuinely free. Total freedom is an impossibility. Total liberty means anarchy, disorder and unpredictability. Freedom at all costs is an excuse for total licence which ends up with each of us doing what seems right to us and everyone pleasing themselves. This is very far from the pattern suggested in the New Testament as it struggles to explain the ways in which we are free and yet freely choose to limit our freedom for Christ's sake.

Limiting our freedom

Paul suggests that we should limit our freedom in various ways.

The *desire to win other people for Christ* should be a limit to our freedom as it was for him. 'Though I am free and belong to no man, I make myself a slave to everyone, to win as many as possible . . . I become all things to all men so that by all possible means I might save some.' (1 Cor 9:19, 22.)

Our *concern for the good of other people* should be a limit on our freedom. Paul expresses this in the light of the slogan we noted before. ' "Everything is permissible" – but not everything is beneficial. "Everything is permissible" – but not everything is constructive. Nobody should seek his own good, but the good of others.' (1 Cor 10: 23–24.) Our freedom ought not to extend beyond what is beneficial and constructive for others. But that limit is freely chosen and self-imposed.

The *consciences of our weaker brothers and sisters* are to be limits on our freedom as well. Paul urges the Corinthians to be careful to ensure that the exercise of their freedom does not become a stumbling-block to the weak. To sin against the weaker brother or sister is to sin against Christ himself (1 Cor 8:9–12). The most sustained treatment of the problems of limiting freedom are to be found in Romans chapters fourteen and fifteen. It is given in answer to the question of whether meat offered to idols – which was therefore cheap and readily available – ought to be part of the Christian diet. Was such meat to be avoided at all costs or snapped up immediately? Paul's complex argument and solution have a significant bearing on Christian freedom and its limits. Christians are urged not to put obstacles or stumbling-blocks in the way of their brothers or sisters. We are urged not to please ourselves, but to please our neighbours for their good in order to build up their confidence in Christ.

Paul's plea to Christians to limit their freedom is summed up in Romans 14:19: 'Let us therefore make every effort to do what leads to peace and to mutual edification.' The Christian's freedom is never an absolute freedom or an excuse for licence. We are not meant to take advantage of our freedom and so abuse it. A proper concern and regard for others and their well-being ought to be a restricting influence and constraint on what we choose to do. Such restraint and constraints are to be freely chosen, and will be by those who truly love and seek to serve God.

Perfect freedom

Those who have entered the kingdom of God have been freed from sin and its power. Yet the paradox is that these same free men and women are being called to choose freely a different life of slavery. This is the way of life which lies at the heart of perfect freedom. Without the voluntary choice of this way of life there can be no ultimate happiness or satisfaction. Paul makes the point in this way:

> 'But thanks be to God that, though you used to be slaves to sin, you wholeheartedly obeyed the form of teaching to which you were entrusted. You have been set free from sin and have become slaves to righteousness . . . When you were slaves to sin, you were free from the control of righteousness. What benefit did you reap at that time from the things you are now ashamed of? Those things result in death! But now that you have been set free from sin and have become slaves to God, the benefit you reap leads to holiness, and the result is eternal life.' (Rom 6:17–22.)

Those who are free men and women in Christ are to become bond-servants of Christ. They are to serve God, to serve Christ, to live for righteousness, and to live for the good of others. All this is to be done for Jesus' sake. They are free from the old law and the openings it created for sin and the ultimate result it brought of death. But now they are to live under a new law. It is the law of Christ and the law of God. It is a law of liberty and freedom. It is a law of love. Paul urges the

Galatians to follow that law. 'But do not use your freedom to indulge the sinful nature; rather, serve one another in love. The entire law is summed up in a single command: "Love your neighbour as yourself." ' (Gal 5:13–14.)

Christian freedom is the freedom to love and serve God and humanity. It is to choose freely to follow the way of life which Jesus lived and witnessed to by his ministry.

PART THREE

Looking at our response

6

Responding to the crisis in society

There is a story about Peter, the apostle and acknowledged leader of the faith. At the height of one of the great persecutions which faced the early church, Peter decided to flee from Rome to the comparative safety of the countryside. On the way he met Jesus. Peter stopped and asked him, 'Where are you going?' Jesus replied that he was going to Rome to die in Peter's place. In the apocryphal tale, this was enough to persuade Peter to turn round and go back to face persecution and death.

None of us likes to face difficulties. We are all very good at escaping from conflict and hardship. Part of the problem is that, when faced with problems, we do not know where to go for help. 'Where are you going?' might equally well be addressed to ourselves as to others in our society. Where can we go to find help in responding to the crises of freedom and authority?

As we have seen, these are not really two separate crises but two aspects of the same problem. Our solution will need to hold together a proper understanding of freedom with an adequate view of authority. In our analysis of freedom and authority, whether in secular and philosophical terms or in examining the biblical approach, it has been impossible to divide the two. For better or worse, freedom and authority are inextricably bound together.

We cannot escape from the situation in which we live. We are modern people living in the modern world and have to come to terms with our society's attitudes and changing values. As Christians we live in the context of the church as well, and face questions of authority and demands for freedom within the confines of our particular religious traditions. We have already made a partial response to these crises by making a critical analysis of the way things are and the direction in which things seem to be going. The danger is that we simply curse the darkness rather than try to light candles. Complaints that things are not what they used to be will not, in themselves, help us to respond adequately to our new situation.

Looking to the Bible

The analysis of this book suggests that we should go to the Bible for an understanding of our current predicament and a creative response to it. But it is perfectly reasonable for folk to ask why we should look to the Bible for help. The answer has two aspects.

First, the New Testament was written and compiled

in a context very similar to our own. It was a time when traditional authority was braking down and individual freedom was on the increase. Politics, philosophy and religion were in turmoil. The old values and practices were in decay and being dismissed. New thinking and experience was challenging the old ways of thinking and living. Traditional authority was no longer simply obeyed without question.

Part of this breakdown was caused by the rise of pluralism. If you walked down a street in any of the cities of the civilized world you would be confronted with a wide variety of religions, philosophies and outlooks – all of them offering the secret of the universe and a golden path to bliss and happiness. The market place was not simply a commercial experience. It was also a market place of ideas and ideologies. Beliefs, and the difference they made to individuals and society, were a matter of hot dispute. One effect of being presented with a wide variety of ideas and outlooks is that we become confused. Which is right and which wrong? How are we to decide between them? Are all ideas and religions equally valid? Is tolerance the way forward? The New Testament church faced exactly the same questions as we do. The answers that were hammered out and written down in response will be a means of insight for us.

The second reason why we should look to the Bible is bound up with the nature of the Bible itself. It is not simply another book; it is God's word. The Bible is God's revelation to us of his will and his way. It carries the authority of God. If we believe that God has spoken in and through the Bible and that his word is always relevant and applicable, then we will want to take very seriously what the Bible has to say. We will not read it simply as an interesting intellectual exercise. If, indeed, the Bible is God's word to humanity, relevant to all times and in all places, and if our human condition is always basically the same, then the Bible must be obeyed.

Challenging the presuppositions

If someone asks you whether or not you have stopped beating your wife you need to think very carefully before you try to answer the question. If you say 'Yes', then it implies that you were a wife-beater. If you say 'No', then it implies that you are still a wife-beater. The problem lies in the presuppositions of the question: you have a wife, and you are or were a wife-beater. Neither of these presuppositions may be true and both may have to be resisted.

The world in which we live operates with sets of presuppositions which are often buried very deeply in the situations we face and of which we are part. Often these cannot be justified but we allow them to stand because we fail to examine them. In Romans 12:2 Paul appeals, 'Don't let the world squeeze you into its own mould . . .' (J B Phillips). This conjures up the delightful picture of children playing with plasticine, squeezing it into different shapes and leaving their distinctive marks on it. The picture sums up so well the danger of allowing the world around us to shape our thinking so that it becomes the only way we understand our world and what to do in it and with it.

The problem with so much of the pressure from the world around us is that it is not obviously wrong. Much of it is good and important – that is why it has such an impact on us. But that does not mean we ought to swallow whole what we are told by the world and its philosophies. Our attitude towards them should rather be, 'Yes, but . . .'

Let us take another look at the situation as we analysed it in chapter one and consider our response as Christians.

The stress on the individual

We have seen how existentialism and its stress on the individual has captured the spirit of our age so well. That picture of the lone individual facing the world and taking on the forces of Big Brother excites our sympathy and support. We see ourselves as individuals who should be able to make every decision by ourselves. This is the pattern for authentic living. What is more, our ability to choose for ourselves, both as individuals and as groups, is fundamental to our Western, democratic style of government. This religion of the Self can be very appealing, and it is of course true that individuals matter. God made us as individuals and gave us the freedom to make choices, but that is not all that is to be said. The well-known line from Donne says that no one is an island. This is what we need to remember when we imbibe existentialist thinking. We do not and cannot exist alone. Existentialism ignores the crucial role of the community in shaping us as individuals. We are born and brought up within a community. We discover who we are only in the context of relationships with others. We define ourselves by contrasting or identifying ourselves with others. We need interaction with others and mutual support if we are to remain alive and healthy. From the beginning of humankind it was clear that it is not good for human beings to be alone. This is not simply some biblical insight which we can take or leave; it is part of our human experience. What it means to be human is to live as part of the human community and in harmony with it.

The mistake is to imagine that being an individual leads inevitably to individualism. We have substituted independence for interdependence. If we are to flourish as humans we need to live and work in harmony and *inter*dependence. It is only from that base and in that context that independence makes sense.

The ability to choose is, therefore, important, but choices cannot be made in isolation from our context or from other people. As a result of the processes of learning and education, being brought up in families and living in communities, our choices cannot be merely matters of individual preference. They are, necessarily, *inter*dependent activities.

The majority

The humanist joins forces with the existentialist in emphasizing the importance of the individual. It is the individual who is free to make his or her own decisions and it is the individual who confers authority on others. The individual expresses his or her own authority by conferring authority on others to achieve what he or she wishes.

But do we really choose who will have authority in our lives? We all tend to dress according to the latest fashion, buy in light of what the adverts tell us and whatever the latest craze happens to be, and we all tend to behave very much as the rest of our particular crowd happen to behave. We are conformists by nature. We go along with accepting the authorities that our peers accept. What is more worrying is that there are certain image makers and opinion formers who remain behind the scenes but deliberately manipulate through the media. We imagine that we are pleasing ourselves; in reality we are conforming to an ideal set up by someone else.

It is very hard to stand against the trend of the rest of society. What we think of as freedom is often a slavery to fashion, to others or to the latest craze.

The Israelites found this out to their cost. When they got to the promised land they found there were Canaanites there already. Living cheek by jowl with others meant that what the others did rubbed off on the Israelites. In the end there was almost no difference between the behaviour of God's chosen people and that of the heathen communities. The call of the prophets was a call to return to God's ways and standards; a call to be different. The same problem exists for Christians today, for we all imbibe the atmosphere and values of the society around us. We allow the world to push us into its mould and we swallow its values wholesale.

If the individual is going to stand against the crowd he or she needs to be able to question in a critical way what is served up by society. All too often we accept the opinions of the press and other media simply because it is published or spoken. We tend not to bother to find out whether or not what is said is actually the truth. It is in this way that we surrender our freedom for the slavery of following fashion and what others tell us to believe.

Of course, this impact of the community on each of us as individuals may operate for good as well as for evil. The company we keep and the things we allow ourselves to be exposed to make a difference. Constant exposure to what is demeaning and harmful reaps its inevitable harvest on our characters. In contrast, constantly opening ourselves to what is good, true, pure, lovely and worthwhile has a beneficial impact.

Our democratic society also shows a much more explicit deference to 'the majority'. The mass poisoning of hundreds of people by Jimmy Jones and the impact of Hitler on a nation and thus on the rest of the world has shown us that authority can all too easily be abused. Our own experiences of authoritarianism lead us to be exceedingly wary about those who exercise authority over us. We seem much happier with exercising our own authority than accepting it from other people. The problem arises when *all* of us opt for our own personal authority, so end up pulling in different directions. Our reaction to this problem in a democratic society is to substitute the authority and will of the majority for our own individual wills and authority.

One drawback with this apparently easy solution is that majorities are notoriously fickle, as the opinion polls show. 'Public opinion', or the majority view, can easily be swayed and manipulated. Another problem is that we cannot guarantee that the majority will always desire what is good and right. Both problems are highlighted in the continuing debate in Britain over whether to reintroduce hanging as a punishments for murder. Parliament has decided time and again that there should be no hanging. The argument is that it would be barbaric and uncivilized to go back to that form of punishment. But it is quite clear from opinion polls that the weight of public opinion is solidly in favour of hanging as an appropriate punishment for some crimes. We need to exercise very careful control over those vehicles which form and shape public opinion. The price of freedom is eternal vigilance.

Majorities present us with two further problems.

Firstly, they are often wrong; truth is not merely a

question of counting heads to see which side has the most votes. Science would never progress if what the majority believed to be the case was accepted without question. It is the individual or small group seeking to discover truth which often overthrows traditional ways of looking at reality. Truth is not dependent on the majority, and can never be.

The other problem is that majorities are always more comfortable with those who are like them. This means that a tremendous pressure to conform is exercised by the majority on everyone else. A certain level of conformity is necessary, but there is always a danger that the majority vote will remove fundamental freedoms of belief. Minorities are always vulnerable to majorities. There needs to be a balance between what minorities are permitted to do and how far they should be required to conform for the good of the whole. Perhaps the real problem is in how we define the good of the whole.

Reason

The humanist takes reason as his ultimate authority and problem solver. Reason is extolled as if it were a neutral tool and as if it provided a standpoint from which we could view the world in an uncommitted way. One of the unreasonable things about this kind of stance is that it often criticizes the Christian for approaching issues from a particular point of view. The Christian clearly has a framework of interpretation and this is dismissed as if it were some kind of cheating. The humanist forgets that his own point of view is just as much a framework of interpretation and that its alleged superiority needs to be established over and against the Christian one. It must not and cannot simply be assumed. The unwary can be conned by this kind of appeal to reason, which is really an implicit appeal to a very particular use of reason based on humanistic assumptions.

Our society seems to imagine that each of us should question everything that we are given, but this is hopelessly optimistic. It presupposes that, though human, we are infinitely perfectable and that our intellectual capacities can be developed almost without limit. Those who teach know only too well how far from the case that is! Of course, human beings can be helped to think better, But we do not have the time, inclination or capacity to think through every single thing for ourselves. It is not only inefficient, but it is unrealistic.

Reason on its own will lead us up the garden path, for we are not solely rational and reasonable. We are emotional and wilful people. Our thinking is often affected by what we feel. I recall a doctor who was speaking with me about the problems of caring for young children whose quality of life was very poor. He was adamant that their lives were worth living. Some students attacked him for allowing his emotions and feelings to influence his rational conclusions. He asked them whether they would rather have a doctor with perfect reason and no feelings, or one whose reason was less than perfect but who sympathized with his patients and felt deeply committed to their good.

Western society is far too optimistic about the power of human reason. Reason has not been spectacularly and unreservedly successful in our modern world. It has certainly produced many wonderful things that we would not want to be without, but it has also produced some ecological and human disasters which are terrifying in their results and implications. Chernobyl and Three Mile Island stand as stark warnings of the potential of nuclear weapons.

Again, humanism's stress on human reason and optimism about human nature needs to be reminded of the tragedy of two World Wars, the continuing struggle for justice and equity in so many parts of the world, and the abuse and disaster which human beings constantly inflict on each other. All the clever thinking in the world has not solved the problems of human selfishness and sin. The world's political, social and economic dilemmas remain.

How then, should the Christian react to this emphasis on reason?

Our capacity to think is, of course, crucial but it is not to be isolated from the rest of what makes us human beings. As Christians we need to do all we can to develop our critical thinking and to learn how to question things. There is for instance, a world of difference between using doubt *in order to arrive at certainty*, which is how the good scientist operates, and the use of doubt *for doubt's sake*. Our critical questions can easily degenerate into scepticism where nothing is believed or accepted, so it is vital that we put doubt and thinking in their proper places.

Reason has not been able to help us come to terms with the market place of ideas we face. In a pluralistic society we are faced with many views of the purpose of life and of right and wrong, and we need help in deciding between these. Pluralism is based on the notion of relativism – the notion that what is true and right varies from time to time, place to place and person to person. Tolerance becomes the be-all and end-all. The concept of relativism is, in fact, nonsense: when I say 'All truth is relative,' I am contradicting myself because I do not believe that the truth of that statement *is* relative! Relativism is also false to the facts for some views are better than others and there are facts which are universal. As Christians we should be using our reason to help us arrive at these better views and universal facts. We should not be using it to sow seeds of doubt for doubt's sake. Our education process needs careful scrutiny to see how we are teaching people to use the critical method and how we help them understand its purpose. Education needs to put truth and the search for truth higher on its agenda.

The Christian goes a stage further in reflecting on the nature of reason. For when we look at the world, the way it is made, functions and operates we discover that it is a reasonable place and operates according to reasonable laws. We, being reasonable, are able to understand the way the world is and how it functions. Science depends on rationality in the nature of things, and on human rationality, to be able to continue. The Christian traces the source of that rationality to God. He made the world so that it is understandable and he made us so that we are able to understand.

This means that human reason and the workings of the natural world are not totally free. They are rooted in the nature of God. We cannot hope to exhaust their full meaning and significance unless we know how they relate to God himself. It is no accident that the development of science in the Western world has been in close relationship with Christianity and been encouraged by it. Science and religion go hand in hand and it is a misunderstanding of the natures of science and religion to make a false dichotomy between them. Neither science nor human reasoning rule out the reality of God, rather they provide many grounds for belief that there is a God.

The individual sets up his or her own reason as the authority by which all else is to be judged, forgetting that this reason is itself a product of other people and the process of education. It is not some glorious individual enterprise, but rather the result of a communal effort. That fact makes it all the more important to expose and evaluate the presuppositions behind what we are taught. The liberal humanist is often deeply critical of Christian presuppositions, but is often strangely lacking in a critical awareness of his own.

Goodness

Humanism believes in the basic goodness of human beings and is optimistic about what people will do if they are allowed to get on with things. However, when people are allowed to do what comes naturally the humanist's optimism is not always vindicated. But the Christian needs to be careful not to overstate the case. There are many fine, good people in the world and one is often amazed at what people are willing to do for the sake of others. Yet there are two things that we need to remember.

First, *God made men and women in his image*, so it is no surprise that there are good people in the world. They bear the marks of their heavenly father. They are like him. The reality of goodness in the world and the existence of some kind of conscience clearly indicates that there must be a source for that goodness and conscience. The reality of goodness cries out for some adequate account of its origin.

Secondly an honest account of the existence of goodness must recognize that such goodness has its counterpart in *the reality of evil.* Humanity's inhumanity is witnessed by the wars, struggles, force, abuse, distress and harm that we inflict on each other. I use the expression 'we inflict' for it is inclusive. If we examine our own feelings and the things that motivate us then the urge to harm others, to get even, to do others down, to succeed at the expense of others, and the warped pleasure we can derive from the pain and discomfort of others, all clearly indicate the existence of something which the Bible calls sin.

Individuals are just like crowds in this respect for, whether on our own or in a group, we are capable of doing harm to others. We say we are free, yet we seem to be the victims of forces that urge us to destroy things, animals and other people. We only have to see recordings of the terrifying rallies of Hitler to witness a crowd being moved to an emotional response which leads to hatred and violence. Wars do not just happen. They stem from human reactions, emotions, needs and aspirations.

If this is the case, then our concern should be to find a way to control and overcome our human nature. The good news of the gospel is that in Christ there is freedom from sin, and the capacity to live in harmony with each other and with the whole of creation.

Rights

The liberal humanist case today seems to focus on the issue of rights. We have seen a growth in the demand for human rights and they now seem to cover everything from the right to work, life, liberty and the pursuit of happiness, to abortion, to the right to have a child by any means, and to express our sexuality in any way we please. We have seen that talk of rights has its problems, but we also need to see that such talk makes the individual the centre of things. Rights tend to be selfish. Of course, there is a proper concern which argues for the rights of others, but even that needs to be focussed clearly on the responsibilities which are implicitly being demanded. Rights do not make sense without responsibility. If I am concerned about the rights of others, I have a responsibility to do something to help them. If I claim my rights to *x*, *y* or *z* then I am claiming that it is someone else's responsibility to look after me and my need.

The Christian has to recognize that in becoming a Christian he or she has taken a responsibility to live for others in the way that Jesus did and taught his followers to emulate. If there are such things as rights, then they stem from the nature of God and his love for humanity, and from human nature and the way that we are meant to live. If there are things that are good for us and other things which are bad for us, then the Christian is to try to maximize the good and limit the evil. From the time of the first human murder, Cain's rhetorical question has made it plain that we *are* our brother's and sister's keepers. We are responsible for them and for how we and others treat them.

This does not exclude a proper responsibility for oneself. Part of what it means to be made in the image of God, and part of what the liberal humanist is pointing to in his account of rational self determination, is that human beings are responsible for what they do and how they live. But this is not simply a matter of pleasing oneself; it is a matter of pleasing God. We are not meant to be victims of our own desires and longings. The freedom to say 'no' to ourselves is as much a freedom as the freedom to pursue what gives us pleasure.

The demand for total freedom can never be realised. It returns us in the end to the issue of authority. By which authority shall we live? Shall we please ourselves or shall we seek to please God? If we choose to live as we please, we shall end up living as the pressurizing world and society all around us want us to live. If we try to please God, then we shall have to seek the ways which will facilitate that and avoid those that hinder. But there is no real gap between pursuing the good of society and our own good; what is rational and good for us as individuals is also what is good for the wider community. God, the ground of rationality and goodness, is the source and end result of the search for both.

Obedience

No community can function unless its members are willing to submit to authority. Obedience lies at the heart of every society. In a sense each individual chooses freely to submit himself or herself to that authority. In reality, we tend to drift into accepting authority and we certainly take for granted the processes which surround us, mould us and shape us. This may be partly because the idea of total freedom is too terrifying for us to cope with. The strain of trying to decide everything for ourselves is so great that we settle for being told what to do, so we submit to a comfortable authority which will look after us in return for our acceptance and obedience. As long as the demands made on us are not too great we tolerate that authority and the consequent limitation of our freedom.

We obey authority because we have found that, in general, it is the best policy. Such free aceptance of authority is good as long as the results are good. Should we then judge an authority on its results? The survival of a society does depend on its government's practice leading to good results. Government, whether of individuals or of communities, is inevitably in the business of consequences. In democratic settings it survives only if the practical effect is good. Good consequences are also crucial if the pattern of obedience is to be confirmed and continued.

The Israelites discovered that obedience to God had good consequences for them; it was not simply a good idea. Good results were the inevitable and right consequence of following a proper way of life. Obedience to God also gave them genuine freedom; they were not simply at the mercy of other people and pressures. Sadly these lessons were often hard and took time to learn.

If we are to obey God's will and way, we must recognize that he has revealed them to us. The early chapters of Genesis reveal that God made men and women to live according to certain patterns – to work, for instance. Naming the animals, tilling the soil, tending the garden, and being fruitful and multiplying all picture God's work-intention for humanity. It is no surprise then that we find that the need to work lies at the centre of the demand for the right to work, and that the experience of unemployment is so devastating.

Marriage is also set in God's creation pattern. Man on his own was inadequate so woman was created to work in partnership and complementarity with man. Men and women are created for each other and are meant to live in a way which expresses that. The leaving of the old family home enables the new couple to cleave to each other, and that cleaving finds expression in the two becoming one flesh, being united as one. The pattern of breakdown in twentieth-century marriage is so far from that ideal that we may fail to recognize what God intended in the first place. We were created to live in a partnership which was for life and exclusive.

This is not a human ideal, it is God's will. Commitment to our husband or wife should be as total as our responsibilties to our parents and children. Marriage and family are basic structures God gives us for living. Opting out is failing to live as God wants.

Relationships between men and women are not disposable. But we do see that some relationships break down. Parents do not behave towards their children as they are meant to and children can also abuse and maltreat their parents. All these relationships are clearly pictured in the Bible as being exercises in mutuality: both parties are meant to fulfil their proper roles. Men were meant to treat their wives in loving ways. Women were to treat their husbands properly. Parents and children were also to behave towards each other as God intended, with love, respect and mutual care. These laws for living have not gone away despite our attempts to live as if they did not exist.

This creation pattern sounds like a recipe for being a doormat in tragic and difficult circumstances. This is not the case. It is a call for a more honest and sustained attempt to live as God created us to live.

We are all faced with certain 'givens' in our home situations. Our families are given and whether we like it or not they are family. What we must try to do is to live as families are supposed to live, with everyone fulfilling their proper roles. We cannot go off and live as if the others did not exist, unless there is mutual breakdown. My fear is that we assume too quickly we have reached the point of breakdown and give up on each other. Instead we should be willing to work at our parent-child, husband-wife relationships, rather than resigning as soon as we face a difficulty. Such difficulties can be opportunties for growth and the deepening of our relationship.

But it was not only at the time of creation that God gave patterns for human living. In the ten commandments human society was given a fundamental basis for its continuing existence. If men and women wish to live in community they must obey certain rules and recognize certain authorities. There need to be proper parent-child relationships. Sexual behaviour needs to be ordered and regulated. Truthfulness must be the cornerstone of relationships. Life must not be at risk and an appropriate way of preserving life must be recognized. Likewise, there needs to be some way of regulating ownership. Our attitude to what is not our own has to be coped with and needs to be constructive. These commandments are not optional extras in the game of life. They are crucial to the existence and well-being of any society. It is no wonder, then, that we find some form of these rules in all societies. We ignore them at our serious peril.

All authority should seek to build on these God-given patterns. Christians are called on to obey those in authority. But there are limits to this delegated authority. In Romans 13 and Ephesians 6, for instance, Paul teaches that those in authority have two limitations.

First, they are answerable to God for what they do. A person in authority can try to live without reference to God but, in the end, he or she will have to give an account to God for the way that authority has been used.

Secondly, those in authority are to act in ways which restrain evil and reward good. Governments are to act constructively for the good of their members. Restraint of evil and reinforcement of good are the keys to that work. If governments fail to fulfil these responsibilties, then they are not behaving according to God's will and our responsibility to obey them can be properly questioned. Likewise, the failure to fulfil the proper roles of parent and child must call into question the right to make the appropriate demands that parents and children can normally make on each other. Mutuality and mutual responsibility are fundamental in all our relationships.

This brings us back to the initial process of struggle and choice. In the name of freedom we may try to reject authority; but if we do we will find we simply end up substituting one authority for another. We are then faced with the basic choice: to pursue our own way or to try to live in accordance with God's revealed will.

We like to imagine that our life is our own and we can make of it whatever we like. Nothing is further from the truth. Our lives belong to God. They come from him and they will return to him. We need to see all that we do, choose and accept in this light. He is the one to whom we are answerable and responsible. His authority is the basis of all authority, but he chooses to allow us the freedom to accept or reject his authority. God is not in the business of forcing men and women to do his will. If his will is not freely done by us, we do not truly do his will. This is the ultimate in freedom. We have the freedom to deny God and our own human nature. We have the freedom to refuse to be our true selves by not living as we were created to live. But the converse is also open to us. If we choose to accept the authority of God in our lives we shall discover that this is the path to genuine freedom. It is a freedom from our fallen nature, from sin, from fear, from the tyranny of ourselves and from the slavery of others. Such freedom is God's gift to all of us, a gift which we have the freedom to accept or reject.

7

Freedom and authority in the church

At the beginning of Chapter One we saw that the crisis of authority within the church is part of a wider crisis of authority in which the demand for freedom is central. However, the crisis of authority within the church has its own special features. With the decline of the traditional churches and the corresponding rise in the house church movement and charismatic groupings, we have to face some hard questions about authority structures and the demand for freedom within the Christian community. The issues are kept alive by our continuing questioning of the fundamentals of the Christian faith – its traditional doctrines and beliefs, the role of the Bible, and the individual's freedom to believe and to question. In addition there is a wide gap between what the churches teach on moral issues and how Christians actually behave, whether it is the difference between what the Pope says about birth control and what many Catholic people do, or the obvious falling short of many Christians from the standards proclaimed by the Christian faith.

The solutions to these problems within the church, and the ways in which the church should respond to the wider crisis in society, will only be found through a proper understanding of the nature of freedom and authority.

Freedom for self-determination

The Christian understanding of freedom begins and ends with God. The free God who freely creates and freely enters into relationship with human beings gives men and women freedom. This freedom is the ability for self-determination and the capacity to make choices. This means that we are answerable to the creator for the choices we make and the results of those choices.

Human nature seems to want to replace obedience to the creator and his created order with a selfishness which puts what we want at the centre, as if we know best. History shows that we do not, in fact, seem to know what is best. Nor are we *able* to do the best thing even when we have an idea of what it might be. What has been described here is *sin* and sinful human nature which replaces God's will with our own human wishes and desires.

The results of sin are catastrophic. They can neither be predicted nor controlled. The exercising of our freedom has serious consequences and we are required to live with these consequences. This is what it means to be responsible. We cannot demand our freedom and then expect to be delivered from the results of exercising that freedom.

What is clear is that God wills our good, and desires that we follow his way. He is able to order events so that even our evil choices may end up being worked for our own good. God's care and love seek to bring good even from our failures, weaknesses and evil. His continuing mercy also works to bring us back into the relationship with him that we were created to enjoy. But we still choose to do our own thing and imagine that we are free to do so, when we are actually in slavery to ourselves, our sinful nature, evil itself, and the forces which seek to keep us captive. Conformity to the world around us is not freedom but another form of slavery.

Freedom to become like Jesus

Jesus came to bring us freedom from all this. He is the liberator *par excellence* and frees us to be ourselves. The problem is that we are not very sure what such freedom is. What are we meant to be and do? The New Testament answer is that we are free to become like Jesus, and free to do what God wants.

The problem with this is that it puts all authority and power into the hands of God. But this makes sense. If God is the author and originator, if he is all powerful, the creator and the source of all authority, then he is to be obeyed, followed and trusted. It is in the coming of Jesus that God's authority is fully and finally revealed. Jesus comes as God's image and representative. He lives as human beings are meant to live. This means that the real issue in both the question of authority and in the question of freedom is what God is like and what Jesus is like.

When a person becomes a Christian he or she may claim to experience true freedom. However, the way that Christians talk about this is often strangely paradoxical. They talk about being slaves of Christ. The New Testament does not talk so much about being a servant as being a slave. To follow in the steps of Jesus is to become a slave to his will and his way. The hymn-writer expresses the thought in these terms: 'Make me a captive, Lord, and then I shall be free.' This freedom is to accept and follow the authority of Christ. It all sounds so simple! One accepts Christ and his authority and then everything is all right! Sadly, this is not quite the case. While life is transformed and people testify to the wonderful change which happens when they become Christians, being a Christian and trying to live the Christian life in the world is not easy. Jesus did not promise that it would be. In fact, he suggested that to follow him was to take up the cross every day and to deny ourselves.

Freedom in Christ is the freedom to follow the authority of God rather than doing our own thing. The problems for the Christian committed to such a way of life are, firstly, how to recognize God's authority and, secondly, how to exercise his or her freedom in Christ. We will look next at how these difficulties were dealt with in the early church, and at the principles we can draw for the church of today from the New Testament letters and records.

Authority in the early church

Recognizing the authority of God

After leaving his disciples Jesus gave them the gift of the Holy Spirit, the Spirit of Jesus. He is also called the Spirit of truth as his task is to lead the church into all truth. The Holy Spirit acted authoritatively in the early church to guide and direct. His authority was God's authority. Naturally the apostles, who had been with Jesus, who had been sent out by him and who had received directly the gift of the Spirit, played key leadership roles in the eary church. Authority was in the hands of those who had been witnesses of Jesus and were now his representatives (see Matt 10:40; John 17:18; 20:21; Acts 1:8; 2 Cor 5:20). The apostle Paul was called to this ministry and, with the others, exercised authority in the early church. In order to build up the church, he and others selected deacons and presbyters, gave orders, prescribed discipline in the name of Jesus, and presented their teaching as the truth of Christ inspired by the Spirit.

The Spirit led the church when it faced decisions. Peter found that the Spirit had acted in a decisive way in the life of Cornelius and then spoken clearly to guide Peter himself to minister to the Gentile community which Cornelius represented. As a result, Gentiles too showed evidence of being filled with the Spirit. Peter's ministry to them broke the laws and traditions of the Jewish people but it was done on the authority of the Holy Spirit. This was clearly confirmed in Acts 15 which records the proceedings of the council of Jerusalem. A letter was written from the council and sent to the Gentile believers, clarifying which of the Jewish requirements were still to be binding on Gentile converts to Christianity. The letter contains the telling phrase, 'It seemed good to the Holy Spirit and to us not to burden you with anything beyond the following requirements . . .' (Acts 15:28). There follow details of abstaining from food sacrificed to idols, from blood, from the meat of strangled animals and from sexual immorality. The Spirit's guidance and the will of the apostolic council are shown here to be very closely linked. The apostolic community confirmed the work and will of the Spirit.

We have come a long way from the times of Jesus and it is hard for us to know what authority we are to accept. The demands of the Bible, tradition, Popes and Bishops, church leaders, synods and assemblies, other Christians and our own confused discerning of God's will, often seem to conflict. This makes life hard! There seem to be two major tests which remain relevant.

The teaching of Jesus

The apostles really had no successors for they received their commission directly from Jesus. The first test for all who today claim to have authority in the church is, therefore, whether their teaching fits with the teaching of Jesus, and is genuinely from the Spirit of God. The way to check is by testing it in the light of scripture.

Conformity with what the Bible teaches is fundamental. Everything we are taught about Jesus, about the nature and will of God, about God's word to humanity and the means of deliverance from the sin which holds us must be tested at the bar of scripture. Without such a test we shall substitute ourselves and our own human subjectivity for the objective word of God which is able to challenge our own thinking and the standards we set and create. This of course presupposes that the Bible is the authoritative word of God. We have already noted that the crisis of authority in the church stems partly from differences of opinion over how much authority should be given to the Bible. However, within the evangelical branches of the church, where the Bible's *authority* is unquestioned, questions of *interpretation* still remain to be worked through. These are issues to which we will return at the end of the chapter.

The example of Jesus

When all is said and done we still require leadership and some human expressions of authority, no matter which form that authority takes. We will continue to put people in office in society and in the church so that we can all function properly. The second test, therefore, is to compare their pattern of leadership or office-holding with that of Christ. The mark of his authority was his willingness to serve those over whom he had authority.

If all authority is given to Christ so that he Lord of all, then all authority is derived from him and those who exercise it are answerable to him for how that authority is used. While it is proper for the rest of us to test that exercise of authority by asking whether it conforms to the pattern and example of Jesus, we need to beware of deluding ourselves. For that question has its parallel in regard to our exercise of freedom. Does our exercise of freedom and our respect for authority conform to that of Jesus?

Problem areas in the church today

It is worth noting that disputes were not uncommon in the early church. Today we tend to imagine that there are more controversies and disagreements in the church than ever before. But though it is no excuse, it is clear that the growth of the church has always been dogged by disagreements and disputes. Often these centre on the extent of Christian freedom and how it may be exercised. The three areas we look at below are probably the ones which cause the most problems today.

Worship

The content and manner of worship is a major area of dispute today. The disagreement is mainly between those who follow traditional, structured forms of worship, and those who advocate 'spontaneous' worship. The first sort is usually led from the front and uses a well-known liturgical form. Its function is a picture of that of the gospel for it seeks to bring men and women nearer to God by its very form and shape. When we do not feel like worshipping God and cannot think of the words to do so, the liturgy and form of worship will help carry us into his presence. The critics of this approach stress the formal, repetitive nature of such worship and suggest that it is less than real, besides lacking warmth and genuine expression.

In its place, they offer a spontaneous approach to worship marked by informal singing, wide audience participation, clapping, the freer involvement of the body in worship, and the exercise of the gifts of the Spirit, especially prophecy, speaking in tongues and the giving of words of knowledge. It is claimed that this style of worship is more immediate and direct and follows more exactly the pattern of the New Testament. Critics of this 'charismatic' style of worship suggest that it is anarchic, frightening for the unbeliever, and can easily degenerate into an emotional experience with no real content and no meeting with God.

One of the reasons why there are different denominations and why churches within denominations vary is that different people find certain kinds of worship more acceptable and comfortable. The fact that we feel at home and able to worship in very different kinds of ways is no reason to belittle our brothers and sisters in Christ or to deny that God can be worshipped in a wide variety of ways. However, we cannot worship in any and every way. There must be limits and these limits must be appropriate to God's nature and to our human nature. They must channel our worship into ways that strengthen and encourage us rather than destroy and demoralize us. The test to apply to any form of worship is to see whether it helps build a people of God who are well grounded in their faith and whose lives bear the fruit of the Spirit of Jesus.

Lifestyle

Christian freedom is not be used as an excuse for bringing harm to our fellow-Christians. This is not only in the matter of worship styles. In the name of freedom many Christians today use alcohol with no qualms at all. Others remain consistently teetotal. This shift in the use of alcohol by Christians over the last ten years nicely illustrates the tension many Christians feel. Is our Christian freedom and its exercise really Christian freedom or are we simply giving in to the pressure to conform to the world around? On the other hand, if we hold on to a pattern of life which was maintained among Christians of previous generations, are we really holding on to what is good for Christian well-being or are we blindly following tradition to make us feel safe?

Leadership

All Christian leaders operate on the basis of some authority and within some kind of authority structure. Some churches emphasize the importance of the office and see appointment to such offices as part of the passing down of authority from the early church to the church of today. Others argue that authority is to be vested in those who show gifts of leadership within the church. Both approaches raise questions about selection and training, yet the difference may be merely between seeing the potential of someone to grow into a role of ministry and leadership, and that of recognizing that he or she is already exercising that ministry or role and simply requires authorization to do so.

Ability, and quality of living

Sadly, we have seen all too many holders of office in the church fail to live up to the standards we know to be required. Television evangelists have been much in the news headlines over their immorality, and the Church of England is still in the midst of heated debate about homosexuality and the priesthood. We do not need to become embroiled in the content of such issues to recognize that people who do hold office in churches and exercise leadership should live exemplary lives. They should be worthy of such office and their character should match their office.

Such people do not need to retreat to the authority of their role and function in order to prove their calling. Rather the sheer quality of their lives and the example of their character should be sufficient when combined with the use of the gifts that have been given to them. The integrity of their ministry should be shown by the fact that there is no gap between what they say and what they do, and this is part of the fulfilment of their ministry.

So those who are called to occupy office in the church are also called to live lives of Christian character. However, this is no more than what is required of every Christian. There is a danger of falling into the trap of having different standards for different Christians. While people outside the church certainly seem to expect higher standards from Christian leaders than from the rest of us Christians, we must avoid that leading to a double standard. 'I do not have to live up to the same level as other Christians', would soon be the excuse for sub-Christian behaviour if we allowed such a division of standards.

There seem, then, to be two elements to leadership. One is the ability to do the job – whether this is a natural talent or a divine gift. The other is the quality of living that should go with such leadership. But in addition, we need to be clear about the context in which such authority and leadership is exercised and the aim and motives involved.

Context, aims and motives

Context is important because the exercise of authority in the church is not the prerogative of individuals so much as the prerogative of the church as a whole. When a church leader speaks, he or she does so on behalf of the whole church. He or she may speak to the church as well as for the church, which means that the church must authorize him or her to do so. There is no room here for self-appointed prophets and apostles unless that prophetic or apostolic role is also recognized and authorized by the church.

Obviously different denominations authorize in different ways and have different rules and regulations for such authorization. In many denominations, women are fully involved in leadership and the quality of their work and living is entirely consistent with such roles. In other denominations it is only men who can hold office. They would not deny that women have a special role, but would make the point that their role is inevitably different. Both groups point to the Bible and the tradition of the church to support their view. We are unlikely to resolve that debate in this book, but what is clear is that all those who are in positions of leadership or authority must have some recognition or authorization by the church of which they are part and to which they minister.

There must always, of course, be room for a prophetic voice to challenge the church and its leaders to be what they are supposed to be. That prophetic message must itself be clearly based on the word and character of God. The person who believes he should speak prophetically must match his lifestyle with the message he brings and show the marks of God's calling to that ministry of prophetic challenge. Only in this way will he have authority within the structures of the church he seeks to challenge.

We need to be clear about the motives at work in such situations. There is no place in the church for authoritarian behaviour, structures and practices. There should be no room for seeking office for the sake of prestige. The pattern throughout Old and New Testaments is that those who exercise authority do so under the authority of God. They are answerable to him both for their call to office and for the way in which they exercise that office. Their characters are meant to illustrate the nature of God and should be conformed to that of Christ.

All leadership in the church should be tested in this way. We should be able to see that God has called a man or woman to that ministry and so be able to endorse that call. There should be an obvious attempt to conform to God's pattern of life, and the character of those who exercise authority in the church should be like that of Jesus.

From this kind of authority, Christians have nothing to fear. When freedom is exercised in such a way, the church has nothing to worry about. If freedom is tempered by such authority, which is under the authority of God, then we will all see how men and women should live. This is surely part of what it means to see God's kingdom come and his will being done on earth as it is in heaven.

Testing authority and freedom

We have looked at the two fundamental tests we ought to use to judge what we do and how we behave: the test of the teaching of Christ, as found in scripture, and the test of conformity to the example of Christ. But there are other, subsidiary tests we can bring in to help our assessment.

The test of tradition

All too easily we do what we do simply because that is the way others around us behave, whether inside or outside the church, or else because that is the way things have always been done. We need to be much more self critical about our way of life and behaviour. We must also ask whether we are simply clinging on to the past in a blind, uncritical way which has more to do with a dead culture than the living gospel. Tradition can be good or bad, and needs to be weighed carefully.

Within the New Testament church there immediately grew up traditions and practices which guided those who came after the earliest Christians and who sought continuity with them. Church traditions were seen as guidelines for judging what was in keeping with Christianity and the mind of Christ. This has continued down through the ages and has been seen as a source of authority parallel to the Bible. Certainly none of us can ignore the way that tradition shapes our thinking and our perception of faith and its implications. Tradition plays a crucial role in making us what we are as Christians. But that does not mean we must swallow it whole and leave it unquestioned or untested. There are good and bad traditions.

The New Testament seems to view tradition as properly authoritative when it fits in with the mind of Christ and is inspired by the Spirit. Some philosophers argue that we can only have one ultimate principle (in this case, either the Bible or tradition) for, if a conflict arises between our fundamental principles, we would be forced to choose one over the other. It is hard to see that church tradition itself could be the final authority in settings of conflict, for tradition always seeks to point back to the example of Jesus and to the ongoing work of the Spirit. It is the Bible which provides the guide to our understanding of these. Unless it is the final arbiter, it is hard to see that our base would be anything but shifting sand.

The test of clear thinking

It is interesting that the Bible does try to deal with exactly the kinds of conflicts we have been examining. Different styles of worship and different attitudes to moral issues in society had to be dealt with in the early church. Paul gives explicit advice on how to deal with issues about which Christians disagree, where Christian freedom has become a divisive issue and where different authorities are being used to justify and bolster one view over another.

In Romans 14 and 15 Paul argues that in matters of dispute each Christian is to be 'fully convinced' in his or her own mind that he or she has taken the right decision. This implies that Christians are to think about things very carefully. We are to use our minds and seek to conform our thinking to the mind and will of Christ. Such use of the mind involves, as we have seen, the questioning of past practice and present pressure from others. Being 'fully convinced' in our mind suggests that our views are not to be held lightly. They are to be the result of considerable mental effort.

The test of accountability to God

Paul goes on to remind us that we shall all stand before the judgment seat of God. It is a proper testing of our freedom to ask whether we would take the same course of action if Christ were present and if we knew that God would ask us for a blow by blow account not only of what we did, but also of why we did that rather than something else.

The test of Christian love

Paul then repeats an argument which he uses elsewhere in disputes over Christian freedom and how it should be exercised. He argues that we must not cause our brothers and sisters to stumble in their discipleship to Christ. We are responsible for their well-being.

What we do radically affects other people and we are never to use our Christian freedom as an excuse for licence and abuse, especially if that abuse harms Christians or others. Paul is not here thinking of trifling details, but of things which so affect other people that they fall away from Christianity. Such action is to be avoided even at the cost of self-limitation. We are not so much in the business of pleasing ourselves and doing our own thing as in trying to please God and ensuring that our own thing does no harm to our Christian brothers and sisters.

The test of shalom

The full flowering of this attitude is found in the final test which Paul suggests we ought to use. He calls on us to test what we do by whether or not it leads to *shalom* – peace or wholeness – and builds up our common life. Paul goes further to say that we need to 'make every effort' to promote shalom and an accurate understanding of God's requirements of us. In other words, this is not just a negative test, but a positive good to work towards.

Our freedom is always limited by the boundaries of God's nature and the expression of Christian love. Yet our recognition of this depends on our acceptance of authority. For the Christian all authority belongs to God in Christ and an understanding of what that entails is mediated to us through the Bible. Many people claim to know the mind and will of the Holy Spirit. They claim that God has told them to do *x* or *y* and that we must therefore support what they say. This is no new phenomenon. The early church faced many such claims and stressed the need for discernment. Claims are to be tested by reference to what we know of God and Jesus. Time and again we are sent back to the Bible because it is through its pages that we gain our knowledge of God. Our conclusions will depend on what we understand the Bible to be and on how we interpret what it says.

Authority and the Bible

The crisis of authority within the church, and certainly many of our disagreements over moral issues, stems back in part to how we regard the Bible. Different attitudes to it have always characterized the history of God's people, from the way the Jews of Jesus' day regarded the Old Testament to the attitudes adopted by different Christians today. These differences must not obscure the fact that all Christians are in some way or other committed to scripture and to taking it seriously in trying to discern what God is saying to his people here and now. Part of what it means to be a Christian is to hold that the Bible is no ordinary book but has authority for the church and for the Christian. The problem is, what sort of authority?

To answer that we must ask two further questions. Firstly, what, if anything, does the Bible claim for itself? Secondly, what attitudes should we, as twentieth-century men and women, adopt towards the Bible?

The Bible's view of its own authority

In Paul's letter to Timothy we find the most explicit claim that the Bible makes for itself: 'All Scripture is God-breathed and is useful for teaching, rebuking, correcting and training in righteousness, so that the man of God may be thoroughly equipped for every good work' (2 Tim 3:16–17). The church down the ages has taken this as sufficient warrant to set up the Bible as the final arbiter in matters of faith and behaviour. The history of doctrinal debate is one of reference and counter-reference to the pages of the Bible. If one side was to make its case then it had to appeal successfully to the Bible. If it was to be countered, then again it was the Bible itself which was basic in that rejection. Tradition supported the Bible's view of itself and recognized the authority of the Bible.

Our view of the Bible's authority

The Bible's view of itself will not be sufficient to convince many who still want to ask what view we should adopt towards it today. Many feel that there is a tension between being a modern, thinking person and believing what the Bible has to say. It is a major issue and it seems that there are two broad approaches that twentieth-century Christians can take. One is to recognize the Bible as being the final authority in matters of faith, doctrine and behaviour, and the arbiter by which we judge what is genuinely part of the Christian faith and what is not. The alternative is to set ourselves up as authorities over the Bible; we become the judges of what is acceptable in it and what may be discarded. If the Bible does not seem to fit in with what we think and feel then it must be adapted to our understanding or set aside as no longer relevant and meaningful. It cannot be allowed to speak for itself and to challenge our approach, beliefs and understanding.

No matter which view we hold, in practice we are all too often in danger of the 'little Jack Horner' method of using the Bible. We put in our thumbs and pull out the plums which we happen to like and happen to agree with – things we believe and find acceptable on other grounds. We are not so comfortable with the rest of the Bible – the cherries, oranges and apples – and would be quite happy to let those bits be forgotten or disappear altogether. We need to be consistent in our use of the Bible. That will require, in turn, some honesty in how we actually view the Bible. Are we under its authority or is it under ours?

Understanding and interpreting the Bible

As evangelical Christians have all we claim to be under the authority of the Bible and to recognize its final authority in faith, doctrine and behaviour. The problem is that we still often differ in our interpretations and emphases. Part of the reason for this lies not so much in what the Bible itself says, but in what we bring to the text as we try to understand, interpret and apply it.

One of the delights of group Bible study is to find that other people soon spot where we are cheating and making the Bible say what it is not actually saying. This is a painful process, but very necessary for we are often unaware of our own presuppositions and the ways that these affect our reading of the Bible. Working with people from other nations and traditions has helped me to spot some of my cultural baggage and to try to see what is actually being said in the biblical text. We need each other's help, whether in a Bible study group or through reading commentaries and using Bible study aids. The community of God's people helps each of us check what we read and understand.

But group study can also reveal different understandings and genuine disagreements over what the Bible says. When we are in such a situation there are two simple things to remember. When the biblical writers set down their message, the message was based on certain theological principles. Situations may change but principles do not. Our task is to get back to these and to make sure that we are reading scripture in the light of them. The other thing to remember is that we must always judge the Bible in light of all the Bible. It is as a whole that God's word is revealed to us. Our Christian responsibility is to search the whole of the Bible and weigh each part in keeping with every other part. We are to balance doctrine with doctrine, one truth with another truth. In other words, we must try to be faithful to the Bible in its entirety and not take one text out of context and use it to support our pet theory. Naturally, this means that there will be tensions, rough edges and incompleteness. But the Bible itself is then the means of working through those problems. It is by going back to it and seeing what is actually said that we will be helped through the maze.

The church has had to recognize that some areas of disagreement are more or less important than others. Agreement is vital on areas of major concern and importance. But there are other areas which are not so central or crucial; different views might legitimately be held about these. How can we judge between what is minor and what is major? The *amount of time and space* given to them in the pages of the Bible provides one test. How *strongly* the Bible deals with an issue is a second test. *What follows* from doing or believing both sides of a disputed area is another. The Bible itself contains some *general rules* for coping with disagreement and we have seen how Paul set these out in trying to help the Romans live with one another. *The creeds* provide a measure for what beliefs are necessary for membership of the church.

If we are open to being corrected and convinced by what the Bible says then we are really under its authority. If we continue to hold our opinion regardless of what the Bible teaches and can be seen to teach then we have set ourselves over the Bible as the final authority.

It is uncomfortable for us to allow God's word to have authority over our lives. But it is the only thing we can do if, on the one hand, we are to be faithful to God and to his revealed word and if, on the other, we are to avoid a morass of subjective, self-centred standards and beliefs. God's authority is true and objective. His word expresses his truth and stands objectively over us. Our proper response is to understand and to obey. Obedience is not so much what we say, but is shown in what we do. Our view of the authority of the Bible is shown by doing God's truth.